Wicked
OMAHA

Wicked
OMAHA

Ryan Roenfeld

THE
History
PRESS

Published by The History Press
Charleston, SC
www.historypress.net

First published 2017

Manufactured in the United States

ISBN 9781540215543

Library of Congress Control Number: 2016956926

To those whose stories never get told.

Contents

Acknowledgements

Special thanks to Chuck Martens and the special collections and archival staff at the Durham Museum, the Dr. C.C. and Mabel L. Criss Library at the University of Nebraska at Omaha and the Omaha Public Library.

Introduction

There's not much left of this Omaha. These days, crowds gather around Tenth and Capitol to get into the Century Link Center to see Black Sabbath or attend a Berkshire-Hathaway shareholder meeting. Today, the home of the NCAA College World Series sits on top of the site of the Union Pacific railroad shops, and tourists gawk at the Missouri River, where a massive lead smelter once belched black smoke. Nearby, a Courtyard by Marriott hotel and Hilton Garden Inn sit on opposite sides of Tenth and Dodge. In 2016, a new twelve-story Marriott hotel was under construction on the northwest corner of Tenth and Capitol, and Elvis Costello was scheduled to play the Holland Performing Arts Center. The Holland now covers Twelfth Street between Dodge and Douglas where the St. Elmo burned up the Omaha night. The Gene Leahy Central Park Mall—a 1970s project determined to take the city back to the river—stretches between Douglas and Farnam from Fourteenth east to Eighth Street. That green space seems a tranquil epilogue to a once boisterous neighborhood, while used condoms and floating fish hint at a history of a different sort.

Unlike the older, irregular origins of Council Bluffs, Iowa, across the Missouri River, Omaha retains a proper midwestern city's somnambulistic grid street pattern. That would seem an obvious layout to anyone confronted with Nebraska's prairie grasslands stretching west to the Rocky Mountains. The city's streets are numbered west from the river, with Dodge Street the divide between north–south streets. Another divide seamed Sixteenth Street, with respectability to the west and all manner of outrage allowed to run east to the river. That

There is nothing left of old Omaha in this 2016 view looking west at what should be Twelfth Street between Farnam and Douglas. *Author's collection.*

free-and-easy attitude dated from the start when Omaha was a mere land speculation schemed up by the Council Bluffs ferry company. That Iowa city relied on fines for gambling, liquor and prostitution ever since the Mormons left Kanesville en masse during the California gold rush. Vice had saved the city and was seemingly exported to the new city of Omaha as an expected and appreciated monthly income.

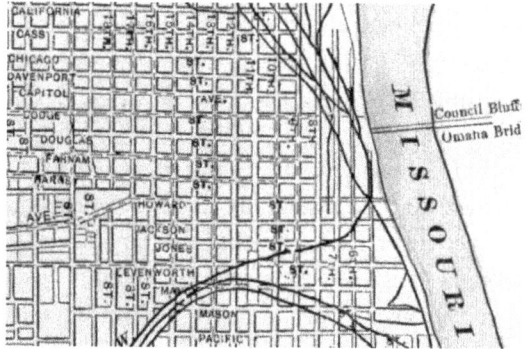

This street map of Omaha dates to 1889. *Courtesy of Archives & Special Collections, Dr. C.C. and Mabel L. Criss Library, University of Nebraska at Omaha.*

Early Omaha was all boom and bust and mud or dust as the Pikes Peak Rush to the Rocky Mountains flooded through and the country's sectional divide

Farnam Street from Sixteenth Street East—1866.

An 1866 view looking east on Farnam shows how humble twelve-year-old Omaha really was. *Courtesy of Archives & Special Collections, Dr. C.C. and Mabel L. Criss Library, University of Nebraska at Omaha.*

turned into the Civil War. Slavery was not unknown in Nebraska Territory, where claim clubs dispensed their own justice. The 1860s also brought the transcontinental railroad and the headquarters of the Union Pacific, which promised permanence and prominence. Likewise, the Homestead Act opened vast western lands and corralled the original owners into ever smaller sections. It was 1865 when the Civil War ended and the first rail was laid to build the transcontinental line west from Omaha. That kicked off a hectic hell-on-wheels of swindlers, gamblers, prostitutes and worse who followed the rails. Nebraska became a state in 1867, and two years later, a golden spike marked the opening of the transcontinental railroad west of Omaha, where one neighborhood in particular became known for vice. Strangers passing through were the favored targets, as Omaha ran wide open and opportunities for women were few and often grim. This era mirrors and contrasts many modernizations as Omaha became a major American railroad center with tracks that connected Chicago, Kansas City, Sioux City and St. Louis to the eastern terminus of the Union Pacific. At the same time, residents were introduced to electricity, telephones, paved streets and water and sewer systems during the 1880s. By the early twentieth century, Omaha was alternately a modern industrialized midwestern city and a place where vice was monopolized by a furniture dealer and political boss Tom Dennison had a finger in every pie. Automobiles headed to California or New York City traveled along Douglas Street and the Lincoln Highway by the time the Albert Law closed down wide-open Omaha.

1

A Rotten System

It was 1870 when Omaha finally grew larger than Council Bluffs, and the Union Pacific moved its headquarters into the Herndon House at Ninth and Farnam Streets. All day long, the railroad steamboats hauled passenger, freight and train cars across the river until 1872, when the Union Pacific railroad bridge opened. Omaha's old riverside docks and landings gave way to a maze of railroad tracks around the Union Pacific shop yards north of the smokestacks of the lead smelter at the foot of Capitol Avenue. It was the neighborhood just to the west that became Omaha's notorious vice district, where the desperate and desperado both sought refuge and often found it.

The newly completed transcontinental railroad brought all of America's hustle and bustle into Omaha. Some travelers found their way to the city's designated district long known as the Third Ward, where morals seemed a matter of profit, political fodder and publicity. Most of these stories are from Omaha's *Bee* newspaper, which primarily served as the political pulpit of publisher and editor Ed Rosewater. Rosewater was a Bohemian Jewish immigrant who came to Omaha as a telegraph operator and worked his way to the top of the city's political hierarchy before his death in 1906. During those years, Rosewater and his newspaper profited politically—and likely economically—from Omaha gambling and prostitution. It also seemed the start of a political machine that would control the city and its vice into the 1930s.

Another constant in Omaha's history of vice was Anna Wilson, the city's best remembered madam. Wilson arrived after the Civil War and

The Herndon House hotel opened in 1858 at Ninth and Farnam Streets and is shown here when it was Union Pacific railroad headquarters. *Courtesy of Archives & Special Collections, Dr. C.C. and Mabel L. Criss Library, University of Nebraska at Omaha.*

was running a Douglas Street brothel by the 1870s. One 1880–81 Omaha city directory listed her operating a "ladies' boardinghouse" at 912–14 Douglas Street. Truly, many ladies boarded there, including Josie Washburn. According to Professor Sharon E. Wood, Washburn was seventeen when she went to Wilson's and stayed the next eight years. Josie later ran her own brothels and eventually provided a woman's view of some of these events.

Gamblers like Anna Wilson's companion Dan Allen were another fixture of Omaha's shadier side, as were confidence men who haunted the train stations and saloons. Swindlers found Omaha and Council Bluffs full of plump prey headed somewhere else, with the additional benefits of jumping state lines and laws. It was April 1873 when the *Bee* newspaper called Omaha the "Headquarters of Professional Monte Players," as three-card Monte—that game of suckers—was brought to town in force by Canada Bill Jones. Canada Bill's exploits would fill their own book, while fellow gambler George Devol considered him a "slick one" who walked around "with the countenance of an idiot." That guilelessness was Canada Bill's greatest asset; who would be taken in by anyone with such "awkward, gawky manners" and "good natured sort of grin"?

A whole host of suckers and the *Bee* noted two sorts of Omaha conmen: some "lay low for large amounts," while others were satisfied by smaller and more immediate sums. The newspaper explained how the "roping-in assistants" hung around street corners to "pick up the green-horns, and steer them into dens" where shills and three-card Monte waited. It was said that any man "carrying a carpet sack is at once spotted by these vultures, and shadowed until they either catch him or that he shows that he is too sharp for them." In Omaha, strangers could not "escape several invitations to drink while walking either to or from" the Union Pacific passenger depot when Canada Bill reputedly had half a dozen bars and hotels. They were all window dressing to fleece the unwary.

The cons and saloons and prostitutes often ran together, and in May 1874 the *Bee* reported the arrest of Annie Morrisey at Amanda Kelly's Tenth Street brothel for robbing a "Dutchman" of ten dollars. The "Dutchman" first visited Jack Shephard's Eleventh Street saloon before he went to Kelly's place. Morrisey threw him out of her room, and that is when he claimed he was robbed. She was back in court a few days later under the usual charge of "being an inmate in a house of prostitution." Her lawyer wanted a trial by jury, but Judge Wilbur was against "calling a jury of respectable citizens to sit upon such a nasty trivial case." Morrisey was set free with a promise to seek "respectable" employment. The scant options available to women in that era seemed to not be a concern.

A *Bee* editorial the next month called it a "Rotten System," in which profiting from vice gave the city nothing but "degrading corruption and unblushing venality." The *Bee* attacked the city marshal by labeling prostitution a "festering sore" that had to be cauterized if Omaha wanted "to restore our police force to efficiency and respectability." The *Bee* estimated 75 to 150 prostitutes in Omaha and pointed out the city charter allowed officials to "restrain, prohibit and suppress tippling shops, houses of prostitution, and other disorderly houses and practices." The charter also made "keeping of, or connection with such disorderly houses or houses or prostitution" a misdemeanor. Anyone convicted faced a fine up to fifty dollars and ten days in jail. The ordinance stipulated it was the city marshal's responsibility on the first of every month to report to the police judge the "names of all persons known to be connected with such disorderly houses" and then file a complaint so the women could be arrested and fined.

The marshals gave their responsibilities to "unscrupulous confederates" and created a system of regulation by "barefaced frauds and high-handed rascality"—effectively blackmail. Marshal Snowden was paid $1,800.00 a year but "delegate[d] the duty" to a favored police officer, while every prostitute paid $7.90 a month to the police court. That fine was divided up: $3.00 to the "school fund," $2.80 to the judge and $2.10 to the "informer." That cheated the schools and prostitute out of $2.10 if Marshal Snowden simply did his job. Worse, the system led to money being "frequently extorted from these women" as "the black-mailing police spy pockets both the fines and costs." The newspaper suggested the police judge knew all about this, with rumors the marshals always got a take. The *Bee* pointed out that often two police officers busted into "a room occupied by courtesans" and forced them to pay the fine "without due process of law." The newspaper called for reform: revision of the ordinance and fines paid only at court. The next day, the *Bee* continued its call for reform and argued against Marshal Snowden and his "bombastic and long-winded set of rules" for the police. Those rules

The meandering Missouri River can be seen in the distance of this early Omaha view looking northeast. Except for the river, nothing in this photograph remains. *Courtesy of Special Collections, Omaha Public Library.*

seemed useless "as long as the old plunder and blackmail" was allowed and "kept up by the Marshal himself." It was "the Omaha social evil system" that corrupted the police as "prostitution is treated as a crime" with only a monthly fine. Money to support the schools instead went to an informer while "money is extorted" that was never recorded.

That same issue printed a letter from Judge Wilbur, who disputed the *Bee*'s assaults on the system. Judge Wilbur reported only forty-nine prostitutes the previous month, and only seventeen paid the "Constable fee" of $7.90. The judge considered Marshal Snowden's appointment of a deputy to handle it "none of [his] business" and pointed out the marshal still made the "required" complaint on the first of every month. The judge explained that oftentimes those brought before him couldn't pay, and it was his decision to give them more time. Judge Wilbur considered prostitution "an evil" that was like liquor and couldn't be "entirely suppressed" in cities. The *Bee* continued its attacks in the summer of 1874, wondering if the marshal knew "one of his policemen 'keeps' one or more prostitutes" and whether those women paid their monthly fine or were even "on the list."

Then the *Bee* received a mysterious letter from someone taking credit for the crime of robbing a black man at the California Wine Rom. But someone had already been arrested. The author might have been Rosewater himself and was printed verbatim—with likely intentional misspellings—as the supposed culprit "[did] not wish to see an inosant person punished for my deads." The letter writer continued, asserting that he was

> the man that made times lively in Omaha with my Six Shooter and now I am rusticating through the countary I play a lone hand and I am a man that the poleace cannot find as I am an old hand at the Business If your city polease wood look out a little Better at night and not hang around Baudy Houses Saloons and gamlen dens they might succeed in captureing the right midnight prowlers but they are to eager to look after a poor Drunk or to Blackmail a poor prostiute insted of watching the movements of thiefs. Eare you receive this I will be far away from hare and as this is a countary of emence distances the oficeres might as well hunt for the nort pole as this chicken.

That July, the *Bee* reprinted an article from the *New York Tribune* concerning Omaha's "queer kind of jurisprudence." The *Tribune* reprint concerned William Taylor, arrested in Omaha as a "suspicious stranger" and then fined three dollars and costs. After that, he was "ordered to leave." The article noted Taylor wasn't doing anything but was "simply 'a suspicious stranger,' and as such ordered to leave, but not before he had, perhaps, made it impossible for him to leave by paying $3 and costs—at least to leave in any other way than on foot." The article believed he was accompanied by Mary Ann Tate, who was released "on promise of a hasty exodus." The reprinted *Tribune* article considered the couple the West's "new Adam and Eve" who "passed out of the Eden of Omaha" and "into the world." Wherever they went, it was hoped they found somewhere "not subject to the jurisdiction of Police Courts like that of Omaha."

A more familiar account in the *Bee* concerned a "belligerent female" in late July 1874 after "Coupon John" Parker had "paid some little attention to a fast girl" called Minnie Evans. That caused the usual problems with his wife, who plotted for two weeks while looking out for Evans. One Friday, Mrs. Parker, "whose traveling name is Nellie Mason," and the "notorious" Tilly Weed tricked Evans to a "secluded spot" near the river. That's where Mrs. Parker "turned herself loose" and gave Evans "an unmerciful pounding," much to Weed's delight. Evans was beat "quite severely" before Mrs. Parker let her go with threats to do worse. Afterward, Evans found a policeman, spent the night in jail and "swore out warrant" the next morning for Mrs. Parker. An officer found her in a "fortune-teller's house" on Eleventh Street where Mrs. Parker was "quite composedly smoking a cigar, and resting easy on her pugilistic laurels." When she went in front of Judge Wilbur, she grew "impudent" and used "very unpretty language" against both the judge and Evans. Mrs. Parker was fined $13.80 and costs but "refused to pay, probably for the very good reason, that she didn't have it at hand" and went to jail for two weeks.

One infamous Omaha dive of the 1870s was Harry Clayton's Crystal Saloon at Tenth and Douglas. In August 1874, William Burgess of Indianola, Iowa, made the mistake of visiting while in Omaha on business. His business was beehives, and Burgess and his business partner were staying at Vandanikers Depot Hotel, where they ran into E.M. Parker. It was Parker who escorted Burgess into the Crystal and upstairs to play faro. Parker lost all of his money—$80 he borrowed from Clayton—and then claimed "his head was thick" and he preferred "a simpler game." With that, "a 'red and black' cloth" appeared on the table, and Burgess lost $108. He went back to his hotel to get some money from his partner, who refused, and then the hotel's owner notified police. Parker, Harry Clayton and Ed Koons were arrested and released on bail. In court, Parker claimed "no such game" was played; Clayton denied the charges as well, claiming it was Koons who "rented and managed" the faro room. David Turner of Denver dealt the cards but wasn't arrested, and "the only game played was faro." Parker's lawyer called Burgess "a humbug and a speculator" who should "have known better" if he played poker for money and asserted the experience "would prove a good lesson for him."

Burgess was called to repeat his testimony, describing "four aces at one end, and in the centre was a jack of diamonds." Marshal Snowden and two officers claimed they didn't know that game. Parker was fined twenty dollars and sentenced to thirty days in jail. Judge Wilbur made clear "it was not his intention to make war upon the 'square' faro banks" that operated "independent and separate from saloons," and Koons was released.

The next month, on September 11, 1874, a recently discharged soldier headed home to Cincinnati was accosted on an Omaha street by a "capper" who claimed to be headed to the same Ohio city. The veteran was talked into the Crystal Saloon for a few drinks and then whisked "up to the faro room" that was "ever ready for the reception of suckers." The veteran lost $150 but went to police after he related his experience to some railroad workers. Harry Clayton, Ed Koons and "a man named Parker" were again arrested and paid their $100 bail while the "capper" remained at large.

One Council Bluffs prostitute named Fannie Rogers crossed the river in October 1874 and "went on a fearful old spree." She was arrested and jailed "but not without making a loud demonstration all the way up." She was let go after she promised to return to the east side of the Missouri River. The *Bee* also called for the organization of an Omaha chess club and told of gambler "Happy Jack" who "picked up a greenhorn from the Green Mountains" named Ethan Alan Priest. Jack "steered him" to the Crystal, and Priest "was induced to play a game of seven up for fun, after he had refused to bite at faro." The "greeny put up $175" while holding three aces on the advice of Harry Clayton but lost when Happy Jack showed off his "flush of three little hearts." Priest filed a complaint that ended with Clayton fined $10 and costs and forced to pay Priest $60 while "Happy Jack" was fined $10 and costs and sentenced to ten days in jail.

A Douglas Street "Shooting Scrape" was in that same issue of the *Bee* after bootblack Tom McVay spent Saturday hanging around Curry's saloon. McVay made the mistake of sticking his nose into a card game and "giving 'pointers' to one of the players." A black man named Henry Turner objected and set off a dispute that ended when McVay "drew a revolver" and shot Turner in the stomach. McVay then ran out the back door, and Turner was taken to a house at Tenth and Capitol. Officers Byrne and Gorman found McVay in a house on the corner of Ninth and Dodge; he was arrested after much protestation but before the police pulled out their billy clubs. The newspaper called Turner's wound "very dangerous" and perhaps fatal.

Before the Union Pacific bridge opened in 1872, steam ferries hauled passengers, freight and construction materials across the Missouri River. *Courtesy of Archives & Special Collections, Dr. C.C. and Mabel L. Criss Library, University of Nebraska at Omaha.*

Omaha remained rife with events along the lines of what happened to Polish immigrant William Fried in November 1877. The *Bee* reported Fried and an unnamed companion traveled from New York City to Omaha, where they found a room at the Eagle hotel on Fourteenth Street. When Fried woke the next morning, his companion was gone with Fried's $475 and a gold watch and chain. Both men were "recently discharged from the Prussian army," and neither knew "a word of English." Abandoned children were also common. A June 1878 report in the *Bee* noted a police officer "picked up a lost boy" with a "little toy wagon" wandering Capitol Avenue. The boy was around two years old, "light haired, [had] on an oil-cloth apron" but had "no hat."

Such varied, troubling incidents would happen over and over, even as expansive new buildings appeared, giving the city a more civilized appearance. In 1879, a new headquarters for the Nebraska Burlington & Missouri River Railroad was constructed at Tenth and Farnam. The old Burlington headquarters is now the only historic building that remains along the north side of Farnam between Tenth and Seventeenth Streets.

2

St. Elmo Variety

Omaha was home to over thirty thousand people when the Poppleton Block was constructed at Tenth and Farnam Streets, south of the Burlington headquarters, in 1880. The boom times seemed endless, with plenty of land available along the eastern edge of the Great Plains and few reminders of its recently dispossessed native owners. There was another sort of Omaha, and in March 1880, the *Bee* reported police picked up Mollie Kernan, Pearl Raymond and Nellie Ross. The newspaper called the women "three bad eggs of the third ward," all arrested as "drunk and disorderly." Raymond's "lover paid her fine," while her companions went to jail. Such was the regular parade through Omaha's police court. That May brought another young man discovered drunk and nearly naked in an alley between Douglas and Farnam. He told police he had been robbed, but after a night in jail, he agreed he was just drunk. The reveler was then fined three dollars and costs. After that came seventeen-year-old Charles Henry, who was charged as part of an "organized band of sneak thieves" who stole silk handkerchiefs and then sold them to the women around Ninth and Douglas. Henry pleaded not guilty and was held for "further examination." Also in court were "two regular tramp attendants" named John Rogers and Charles Bisbee who had been out of jail for only two days. The pair were "given the full benefit of the tramp law" and sentenced to twenty days in jail. At the end of that day's session appeared "two prominent citizens"—John Smith and John Doe—who went "on a jamboree" that ended in jail. Smith and Doe paid the usual three dollars and costs and were released.

While Farnam Street was Omaha's main commercial district, the commerce in the neighborhood a block north was something very different. *Courtesy of Archives & Special Collections, Dr. C.C. and Mabel L. Criss Library, University of Nebraska at Omaha.*

All sorts of Omaha jamborees occurred after Jack Nugent's St. Elmo "variety theater" opened in the spring of 1880 at 104 South Twelfth Street in the block between Dodge and Douglas. As mentioned in the *Bee* on May 8, a visitor "thought he would take in the city" and its many saloons before he "struck the St. Elmo." The man was "entranced with the novel performance," and then he was discovered by police in a nearby alley and taken to jail. At court, the man told Judge Hawes he had been robbed of his watch and chain and sixty dollars. The newspaper figured "he was so intoxicated that robbing him was probably a matter of little difficulty" and thought he had "learn[ed] a lesson" and would not carry so much the "next time he goes on an exploring expedition in a strange city." The St. Elmo quickly earned a reputation as a paradise for those prone to plunder strangers in the city.

Another prostitute named Jane Davis made her way into the *Bee* at the end of May after she "took too much 'tea' and made things lively." A police officer "dragged the noisy creature" up Dodge Street until they got to the Metropolitan Hotel at Twelfth Street. Then, Davis lay "down on her dignity" and refused to move. She was taken to jail by carriage after being "rather unceremoniously rolled" inside and the officer "sat down upon her." The newspaper predicted Davis would have time "to reflect on the uncertainties of gin and water." One "bad man of the Third Ward" was William Burke, who was arrested for assault and battery. According to the *Bee* in June 1880, Burke "knocked down a Swede in front of Barney Shannon's saloon Sunday, for no apparent reason" except he liked to fight. He was fined five dollars and costs.

The "state of things" around Omaha seemed clear in a June report by the *Bee* from an unnamed census taker on what he found in the city's Third Ward. The newspaper noted the neighborhood was "not particularly famous as the abode of refinement or intelligence" despite some of Omaha's "best citizens" living there. The census taker quickly admitted difficulty from the neighborhood. Residents proved "very suspicious" and considered him "an informer of some kind, in the employ of the police, or, at best an agent of some sort." He encountered "many abusive people" who insulted him "with epithets of no flattering nature." As that was not a neighborhood of early risers, the census taker woke up some folks "in no very pleasant humor" with the door "slammed in my face with a curse for being a d——d peddler, disturbing decent people at that hour of the day!" Sometimes the man met people who didn't know where they were from or how old they were, and he acknowledged "a number of houses of questionable repute." Residents tried to evade the questions "or answer…in an equivocal manner" until they were reminded of the penalties for refusing to answer. As for their occupations, "Oh, they are all dressmakers." Suspiciously, during the first three days he listed four hundred to five hundred names but not "a single case of death during the present year," as he found "considerable dirt, but strange to say, no cases of sickness."

In late June 1880 came a brief blurb in the *Bee* that authorities would run out the "houses of ill-fame" near the Dodge Street School at Eleventh Street. The particulars followed on June 22, with the *Bee* reporting nearby brothel owners were notified along with a "lively rumpus" after a couple "women of the town" enlivened Thirteenth and Dodge. The two women were Lizzie Johnson and Nellie Ross, both "raving drunk," who made the night "hideous with their noise." On the way to jail, the two women were "howling like demons all the way" as a crowd gathered to watch the spectacle. The *Bee* referred to them as old-timers.

Altogether, there were fifteen prostitutes noted by the *Bee* who all lived near the school and were arrested late the next night. They were "lodged in the luxuriant quarters" in the courthouse basement for violating the ordinance against "houses of ill-fame" within two blocks of a school. One

An unnamed Omaha woman. Most of the women in this book never used their given names. *Courtesy of Special Collections, the Durham Museum.*

of those arrested was a woman who was accompanied at court by a little boy about three years old. The woman said she owned the property, "kept no prostitutes" and "refused most emphatically" to leave. Most of the other women told the judge they had not had time to "look up new quarters." All cases were dismissed for three days "with the understanding" they would better find somewhere else or face the "extreme penalty."

How women found their way into these circumstances varied, with one path outlined by a Mrs. Pratt in the *Bee* on June 24, 1880. She was found guilty of adultery after she and her lover John Griffin were arrested in an apartment above a Douglas Street restaurant. There is always more to every story, and during her court appearance, she told a tale that "moved the hearts of every occupant." Mrs. Pratt told the court she married Mr. Pratt, a carpenter, in 1878 and "lived happily" until he was "stricken with paralysis." Their child was born soon after and proved to be "entirely helpless." Some months after unsuccessfully trying to care for her husband and child, the "despairing" woman left her husband with the county and sent their child to her parents in Iowa. That is when she entered one of Omaha's "houses of ill fame." The helpless Mrs. Pratt found herself "sick" in a "Gilded Palace of Sin" until she met Griffin. She was released, but Griffin remained in jail for "further examination."

Excitement around the St. Elmo "varieties" continued in late June 1880 after one of Jack Nugent's employees was arrested for drunkenly disturbing the peace. The *Bee* reported the man attempted to "resist the officer" and was "frustrated by a thumping of the guardian of the peace." The next day, the *Bee* noted two "fallen women" were arrested for being drunk. The pair were "carrying on their nefarious business in apartments in the old 'St. Elmo' building" and fined one dollars and costs. Also in court was "Teddy" Heuth, a St. Elmo employee who got drunk Sunday night. He grew "violent in his demonstrations and abusive in his language" and threatened passersby until he was arrested near the corner of Twelfth and Douglas. The police officer gave Heuth "a chastisement" before he consented to the "inevitable 'come along now.'" That was not Heuth's first time in trouble, but previously he had it easy "on account of his many friends and profuse promises of reform." On that occasion, he was sent to jail for thirty days. Also drunk were Gilmore Barr and Henry Coup, who "imagined themselves" members of the police in another example of abuse. The newspaper thought they should have "arrested each other" but instead made "a raid upon a house of questionable character" on Douglas Street. There they tried to use their cigars to burn the women and "otherwise abused" the female inmates. They were fined five dollars and costs but couldn't pay. They were sent to jail.

There was "a woman at the bottom of the trouble" in the *Bee* on June 30 after a shooting on Twelfth Street startled folks. A crowd gathered to discover a man named McKee shot. He used to bartend at the St. Elmo and had been fighting with someone "said to be Charlie O'Connors." During their dispute, O'Connors reputedly pulled his gun to shoot McKee, but the intended victim grabbed O'Connors's hand and "turned the ball in another direction." O'Connors shot again, and one bystander claimed that it was the shot that hit McKee, even as McKee said it was the third shot fired. Either way, McKee was hit in the left leg, and the bullet lodged in his knee. Medical aid was sent for, and McKee was taken to a home on Capitol Avenue. Billy Moran and Henry Parrish were hauled in as witnesses while "all accounts" indicated this "trouble was about a woman." O'Connors was said to have fled through the St. Elmo and shouted out, "I've killed a man!" as he escaped. The police were still looking for him.

A less bloody dispute over the St. Elmo took place between Omaha mayor Champion Chase and Judge Hawes, who threatened to charge the mayor with contempt. During court, when Judge Hawes was in the middle of "trying a case of disturbance of the peace," he was interrupted by Mayor Chase. The mayor turned to leave, but Judge Hawes suspended court, as an "excited" mayor meant "something important was in the wind." Mayor Chase told the judge of "continued complaints from everybody in the town" about the St. Elmo, and it seemed "they could not get anything done by the officers or the judge."

Judge Hawes pointed out that no complaints had been filed against the St. Elmo but noted that Nugent, the owner, had been fined. The judge also "heard that Jim Connolly had whipped his woman, and raised quite a row down there," but no one filed a complaint. The judge was unable to do anything until a complaint was filed and "suggested that the mayor might do so if he saw fit." The mayor "replied pretty sharply" that everyone complained of the St. Elmo and insinuated that Judge Hawes was "in cahoots with the St. Elmo crowd." Those were sharp words directed toward Judge Hawes in his own courtroom, and he "rose upon his official dignity" and said "any more such language" would end in a charge of contempt and jail. Mayor Chase claimed to be "ready to go to jail for three or six months any time" but would "protect the honest yeomanry of this country at all hazards." Political grandstanding is nothing new, and after more heated words, Mayor Chase left the courtroom, followed by a reporter. The *Bee* quoted Mayor Chase concerning the "continual charges made…against the St. Elmo theatre." According to the mayor, "hardly a night" went by without someone "swindled or robbed." Mayor Chase proposed to close the St. Elmo, had told Nugent that to his face and would "clean out the whole outfit, police judge, city marshal and all."

To Mayor Chase, "the idea of a man I permitted to be a police judge" throwing him in jail seemed "no better fun." The mayor suggested that the reporter go find George Linde for the "latest outrage," while Judge Hawes claimed to know nothing about it. Judge Hawes told the reporter "there was no doubt" the mayor "was crazy and had been for two years." The reporter tracked down Linde, but his account proved poor. Linde had no complaint against the St. Elmo except a possible incident concerning a man who was "about his place" on Tenth Street. Another man said to be associated with the St. Elmo followed the first man "like a dog" herding sheep to slaughter. The pair headed toward Douglas Street, and the first man ended up in jail "without a cent" and claimed he had only had "one drink of whisky that took away his senses." Linde said he didn't know if the St. Elmo was involved.

At the end of July 1880, a "Prostitute's Plunge" was described by the *Bee* as an "involuntary bath" in the "Big Muddy" one Sunday night. Apparently, a pair of "well-known women of the town" named Nellie Brown and "Pinkey" Grey drank all day before they decided to visit to the river. The two women "found two barges and a small skiff anchored to the rip-raps," but when they tried "to step from the barge into the small boat" trouble arose. Brown and Grey both found themselves "struggling" in the fifteen-foot-deep river "the color of well creamed coffee." The two grabbed on to ropes but could not pull themselves out. A Union Pacific watchman named Peter Kuhn "rushed to the rescue" and pulled Grey out of the river while she was "hallooing like one possessed." She continued her outcry with shouts of "Save Nellie!" J.C. Heimendinger saved Nellie, risking his life as "she threw her arms about his neck and nearly dragged both to the bottom." Then Mike Meaney showed up and—"not to be outdone in bravery"—jumped into the river to save a dog that belonged to Brown. That was after the dog

A modern view of the Poppleton Block, built in 1880 at Tenth and Farnam Streets, now home to the Omaha Convention and Visitor's Bureau. *Author's collection.*

"had sunk for the seventh and last time." The plunge into the river "brought the women to their senses," but they "seemed inclined to view the accident in a humorous light, as they started to walk home in their soaked attire." The newspaper reported Nellie Brown lived at Tenth and Douglas and Pinkey Grey on Dodge Street.

Then, in August 1880 came a sudden "Raid upon the Faro Banks and 'Gilt Edged' Houses." The newspaper considered this a "peculiar and sudden change in the atmosphere," as such a raid hadn't happened in a decade, and the *Bee* predicted it wouldn't happen again in as many years. As it was, Marshal Westerdahl and four officers headed out at ten o'clock one night "to go out and bring in some tramps." The marshal "had a big scheme in his head" and set out north from Twelfth and Farnam. The posse's first visit was to a faro bank where a motley crew of eighteen men were busy "bucking the tiger," and the felonious cardsharps were escorted outside. The marshal's next stop was "Dan Allen's place," where he and his men found Allan and Goodley Booker playing cribbage. Allen asked the marshal what he wanted and was rebuffed by a brusque "None of your business....I want you to come along with me." The pair was added to the eighteen outside. With that, "the march resumed," and another ten men were added from Higgins's saloon on Douglas between Twelfth and Thirteenth Streets. The *Bee* reported "no kicking anywhere," although at Higgins's "the dealer very naturally tried to secure a dark leather wallet which the marshal seized." It contained fifteen "golden double eagles" worth $300. The marshal and his officers also confiscated "drawers, boxes and cards," and Officer O'Donohoe had his arms full of items liberated along the way.

Two more police officers joined the march to the city jail at Twelfth and Douglas, yet "half the captives" managed to sneak away and only sixteen of the thirty suspects arrived at jail. Fifteen of them gave "the namesake of Pocahontas' fickle object of affection," as the jail "probably contained more of the Smith family to the square foot than any other equal area on the face of the globe." The throng of wrongdoers called for a judge so they could make bail, while the marshal and his men went back and "raided the various houses of ill fame" along Twelfth and Douglas to bring in twenty more malcontents. By two o'clock in the morning, most of them bailed out. News of that night's crackdown hit the St. Elmo and "produced a scene of indescribable panic and confusion." Patrons "fled incontinently" as Twelfth Street went "from a blaze of light" to "a tomb of darkness in the twinkling of an eye."

There was nothing but a sad shame for one woman in late August 1880 in what the *Bee* described the "Last Flutter of a Poor Soiled Dove." It was

Councilman W.H. Roddis who alerted authorities to a woman "in a sick and very destitute condition…lying in the weeds and mud" underneath a railroad trestle on the south side of town. The police sent a wagon to carry her downtown, where Judge Hawes sentenced her to the county jail. This was the same woman who had been found near the gasworks and sent to jail. The *Bee* described her as "the most utterly wretched looking object a human being has ever looked at and resembles rather a half-putrid, animated corpse than a living person…rotten with disease and her looks and condition beggar description." The newspaper claimed she was sent across from Council Bluffs, but Omaha authorities sent her back. The *Bee* did not express surprise at her Omaha reappearance and noted she didn't seem to have long to live. Judge Hawes sent her to county jail instead of the city lockup, as he thought "she would die in that filthy hole before night." The sheriff didn't want her in the county jail either and claimed it was full. It was more likely "she was such a horrible object to care for." Judge Hawes considered it "a shame that there was no place to which she could be sent and cared for, and so it was." What was needed, the judge said, was an Omaha city hospital.

Throughout the discussion on her fate, "the poor creature, the wretched object of their unwilling care" was left in the back of a wagon "in the middle of the street," It was August, and the woman "did not raise her head or show any signs of life." Her clothes were "wretched, filthy rags" that gave little cover from the sun's "scorching rays." A "crowd of gaping boys and men" looked on with expressions of disgust, and even the *Bee* reporter "was heartless enough to wonder if she wouldn't die before time for the paper to go to press and thus help him out." The newspaper sermonized that if her "erring sisters" had seen her they would be "chilled by the horrible spectre of the creature whose counterpart the best of them are likely to become." The unnamed woman was eventually taken to the poor farm.

The disreputable spectacle was not viewed by everyone with a nudge and a wink. One story in the *Bee* on September 10, 1880, concerning women and the law, noted that the Woman's Christian Temperance Union had petitioned to enforce the "Sabbath laws." This effort forced city officials into an uncomfortable position. Previous attempts to enforce the Sunday closing laws were stymied by legal language as to whether or not "the disturbance of the peace and tranquility of the city" were actually violated. In the end, "everything fell to the ground after a single spasmodic attempt," as the judge preferred a monthly fine "from the women and gamblers," not one every week. With that, the attempt to close Omaha's saloons and bawdy houses on Sunday "ended in another grand fizzle."

This modern view from Eleventh and Dodge Streets offers no indication of the bawdy houses or saloons that once occupied the area. The Holland Arts Center now occupies Twelfth Street and the site of the St. Elmo. *Author's collection.*

The *Bee* then pointed out that by law the mayor and marshal were still compelled to enforce the prohibitions against "any person or association of persons who shall permit in his, her, or their house, out-house, yard, or other premises under his, her, or their control, any gambling with cards, dice, or other implements or devices used in gambling." The always helpful *Bee* pointed out the relevant section of the city code:

> *Any person or persons who shall keep a house for the purpose of gambling therein, or who shall suffer or permit other persons to come there, or permit other persons to come there, or to frequent and come together there…and any person who in any public place shall play for money or any valuable thing at cards, dice, or in any other manner, or shall bet at faro, keno, or any other game.*

Omaha law also supposedly made it clear that it was a misdemeanor for anyone connected in any way to "any house of prostitution or other disorderly house," including property owners who rent to "any notorious prostitute." All the law required was for two or more people to file a written complaint with the marshal that "any house or place in their immediate neighborhood is openly and notoriously kept or maintained as a house of prostitution or disorderly house." That was it. That was all it took. The *Bee* called for "officers to cut out this report of the committee and the ordinances quoted, paste the same in their hats and recall their oath of office to mind." Of course, the de facto system would continue for decades regardless of the law, which served mostly to score political points.

On September 21, the *Bee* announced Omaha was "After the Girls Again." This time it was a Sunday, and a "considerable sensation" arose in "Hell's Half Acre" after the marshal and his officers raided the Gold Dust saloon at Twelfth and Dodge. Police were "stationed at every door," while four women and ten men—including the owner—were rounded up and taken to jail. It was ten o'clock at night when Judge Hawes convened court long enough to accept bail or otherwise hand down his judgment. The raid spread fear along the street, but no more houses were pulled.

A few days later, on September 25, the *Bee* concerned itself with a new troubles in Hell's Half Acre as an "immense crowd of visitors" had arrived in Omaha—a "full quota of sporting men and hard characters." Although there were few reports of robbery, the newspaper thought most wouldn't be reported. On Thursday, Omaha's saloons, faro banks and sporting houses were busy and crowded. Among the reported incidents were "two countrymen" who paid a visit to a Twelfth Street "bagnio." After one drink, one man "became insensible," so his friend went to find some way to haul him home. However, he was "half out of his senses himself" and couldn't recall the place where his friend had obviously been drugged. According to the newspaper, the unnamed man was "still on the hunt" and claimed his companion carried "a roll of money and a gold watch."

Among the crowds that filled Omaha's pleasure mills were the soldiers stationed at Fort Omaha. That installation had a presence in the city since the late 1860s. When it served as headquarters of the U.S. Army's Department of the Platte, it was filled with the soldiers who fought in the Plains Indian Wars. In early October 1880, the *Bee* listed "several war widows among the demi-monde" after Company H of the Ninth Infantry shipped out. The soldiers were headed to Fort McKinney near present-day Buffalo, Wyoming.

The death of actress Kitty Matthews was announced in the *Bee* in November 1880 as the "Curtain Rung Down on the Last Act" and brought out the "fraternal feeling" among Omaha's "theatrical people." Matthews was twenty-four years old, born in England and came to America "a serio-

These five unknown Nebraska women were photographed around the turn of the twentieth century. For some, the allure of Omaha's bright lights led to exploitation and worse. *Courtesy of Special Collections, the Durham Museum.*

comic singer." She arrived in Omaha in April for a four-week stint at the St. Elmo. She got sick after two weeks and died six months later. It was said "her friends among the professionals" cared for her, and Jack Nugent was singled out for his "big, warm heart." The night of Matthews's death, Nugent made sure the St. Elmo stage was decorated with the chair she used; it was "draped in mourning…[with] floral tributes." The vacant chair was at the center of the stage when the curtain rose that night, and stage manager Harry Parker offered the crowd a tribute to Matthews. There was "not one unmoved person in the house" when Parker finished with "Let the Dead and the Beautiful Rest," sung by Minnie Lamont. Matthews's funeral was well attended, with a "long line of carriages" to the cemetery.

The next month, Nugent bought the Academy of Music in Council Bluffs, but the *Bee* figured the St. Elmo would "be run as usual." In December, Billy McKee was in charge at the St. Elmo, but he was arrested over two nights' worth of receipts that vanished. Nugent closed up the St. Elmo himself in early January 1881. The *Bee* noted this was only "temporarily for repairs," and he planned to reopen with "an entire new company, new scenery and auditorium" and everything "first class." Still, the mayor ordered the St. Elmo closed on Sunday nights in March. The next month, on April 7, the newspaper reported a Tuesday night fight at the St. Elmo: "John Walton played the heavy tragedy part and fired Mike Gilligan through a front window on the walk." Walton was hauled off to jail, and it required "united efforts" by the police to get him there. That was the year of the great Missouri River floods that created Lake Manawa, and on April 16, the *Bee* reported Omaha police must have a "peculiar and touching respect for the dead," as a dog had been decomposing on Douglas Street for two weeks despite several complaints having been made "to wearers of the blue." A familiar notation in May 1881 concerned one Monday at the St. Elmo with "a full house" that included members of the military as "things generally hummed." That month, Nugent got married in Council Bluffs to Nellie McCormick, a St. Elmo actress.

There was news of some good deeds in the disreputable district on June 28, 1881, with a "gala day for the Omaha mission" for three hundred hungry children who left the school at Tenth and Capitol to spend the day at Hanscom Park. The newspaper asked the city's "kind-hearted" to "send some cake or sandwiches" and requested transportation "for an hour or two in the morning" to let the disadvantaged have "one day of fresh air and fun."

Fire was also a frequent visitor to early Omaha, and at the end of July 1881, there was "Wild Excitement" in the *Bee* after a lantern exploded at

Department stores and fancy business blocks lined Farnam east of Sixteenth Street when it was Omaha's primary commercial corridor. *Courtesy of Archives & Special Collections, Dr. C.C. and Mabel L. Criss Library, University of Nebraska at Omaha.*

the St. Elmo and set fire to the stage curtain and a tapestry that hung from one of the theater boxes. The theater was filled "to its utmost capacity," as was the adjacent saloon. It was the stage manager who tried to "darken the stage for scenic effect" but instead knocked a lamp over, and it blew up when the oil caught fire. The fire brought a "scene of fright and confusion" as the crowd rushed the door back into the saloon. In the scramble for the exit, "many climbed upon the heads and shoulders of those in front of them" and trampled the fallen. Someone threw a chair out a second-story window, and it "was followed by a stream of humanity" that that didn't end until the St. Elmo was empty. Some of those who fled out the broken window were "cut by the fragments of glass and hurt in falling upon the walk below, as they were crowded and pushed by those behind them." The "ballet girls screamed in terror" and ran from the stage through the wine room and then out into the crowd, still wearing "their scanty stage costume[s]." The newspaper claimed "some of them cried for their lovers, others for their pet dogs, and others still seemed to scream because they enjoyed so doing." The St. Elmo fire was soon put out with water. Someone rang the fire alarm at Thirteenth and Douglas, and Engine No. 3 raced from the Farnam Street fire station. The firefighters discovered that the fire was already out as they turned the corner onto Twelfth Street.

The woman dubbed "Kansas City Liz" made her way into the *Bee* on July 22. Her real name might have been Elizabeth Foster, and the headline read "Three to One." Around 2:30 a.m., John Eagan, Charles Tracey and Fred Hughes went "prowling about the streets" and "proposed to 'go on a tear.'" They went to the corner of Twelfth and Dodge and the home of a "woman of variegated reputation" dubbed "Kansas City Liz." She was by herself and hid behind the door when the three men demanded entrance. After she told them to leave, they kicked in her door. Kansas City Liz responded by picking up a chair and beating them "promiscuously about the head." One of the men hit her in the face—breaking her teeth—and with that she ran out into the street "screaming murder." Two police officers happened to be nearby and arrested the three men. Eagan was let go after paying five dollars and costs, while Hughes was sent to jail when he couldn't pay his six dollars. Tracy was set free "because nothing could be proved" other than he was "in the crowd." However, the *Bee* noted Tracy visited there the night before, and Liz had busted "a water pitcher over his head" when he wouldn't leave. At the end of trial, Liz assured everyone that she'd purchased a "dessolver, an' if a man she didn't want [to] come 'round her house he'd git [the] daylights blowed outen him."

At the end of that August came the unusual news in the *Bee* that the saloons were closed, and on Sunday, the "streets of Omaha were thoroughly dull." With Omaha all closed up, everyone went over to Council Bluffs, where a reported five men were kept busy "handing out foaming lager to the thirsty crowds" at the Union Pacific Transfer depot. The *Bee* also noted "several places" out near the racetrack were "besieged," and one small Iowa brewery "sold every drop of beer early in the afternoon" as "many in desperation took whisky."

Otherwise, times seemed normal enough by October 1, 1881, with the *Bee* headline "Drunk, Fight, Jail." That was the fate of an unnamed Iowan who visited the St. Elmo for a drink and then grew belligerent. The Iowan singled out Mike Gilligan and wanted to see him out back. That is where Gilligan "pummeled his antagonist to the latter's content." Officer McCune happened by, and the Iowan "was carried away in a cart" to jail. Then one "reduced thespian" named John McDonald found himself charged with robbery in district court in the middle of October. McDonald was allegedly an actor who "perform[ed] at the St. Elmo." He rolled twenty dollars from Jack Connelly, alias "Whiskey Jack," who was spread "on a sidewalk in his usual condition of elaborate intoxication." Connelly had recently been paid a month's wages by the Union Pacific and had almost forty dollars. McDonald admitted on the stand to taking twenty dollars, but the jury still found him guilty of grand larceny.

One actual feature of daily life of the "Omaha nymphs" was featured by the *Bee* on October 22, 1881. The newspaper considered "one of the most strange and superstitious practices" common among "morally loose" women was that almost all of them "burn[ed] incense in their houses to keep away bad luck and misfortune." One reporter consulted a "prominent druggist" who said burning incense was "almost universally indulged in by the women of the town." The incense made up "an important branch" of his business and was "very expensive, as they are imported from distant countries." One ingredient was "olibanum"—otherwise known as frankincense—and the other was "dragon's blood," from the calamus palm grown on the island of Borneo. The two "drugs" were "properly mixed and prepared for this particular use, and while burning will admit a peculiar fragrant odor." The newspaper considered it "useless to conjecture" where "the custom was derived by this class of people." However, the women "have the greatest faith in its efficacy as a means of averting evil and sickness of all kinds."

In December 1881, the *Bee* called on Omaha to reform, as the city had a "hard name abroad." It was said that "life and property are not secure," and the city was "infested by roughs, rowdies, thieves and thugs." All of Omaha's "commodious public schools, costly churches, palatial hotels" meant little compared to the "dens and disreputable resorts that flourish in the very heart" of the city. The newspaper placed blame on the mayor, as it was "his sworn duty to break up every resort where men and boys, roped in by indecent shows, are maltreated and robbed." It was the mayor who should "suppress vile dens where bloody brawls and murderous affrays" were common. It seemed a "disgrace of this city such disreputable places have been tolerated undisturbed" and the mayor did nothing. Omaha's Irish-born Democratic mayor James Boyd told the *Bee* he believed "keepers of the low dives and disorderly houses would fail to secure the necessary bond and could not get thirty freeholders to endorse their application." The mayor intended to enforce the Slocumb Law after the New Year "at all hazard" and actually impose restrictions on the sale of beer and whiskey in Omaha.

The *Bee* congratulated Mayor Boyd "for sustaining law and order" and then called out the evasion of "notice of publication required." The newspaper claimed the mayor would "license every applicant that files the necessary papers and pay the $260" regardless. The licensing board was made up of the mayor, a city clerk and president of the city council, and it appeared obvious "whatever Mayor Boyd rules will be sustained by the clerk, and two being a majority Mayor Boyd will control." All the while, "keepers of some of the most notorious dens of infamy" applied, including Jack Nugent of "the St. Elmo, where hundreds of our young men have been ruined and drawn from the path of decency and honesty, and where, as is well known to our city marshal and police, men are frequently beaten and robbed." The *Bee* claimed no one "dares to file" against the St. Elmo "because it might cost him his life." The newspaper considered it "monstrous" when respectable citizens were threatened or tolerated by "criminal resorts." The newspaper questioned whether Omaha was a "frontier mining camp or a metropolis," as it truly seemed a bit of both. A *Bee* reporter was refused when he went to the city clerk to retrieve the "names of the bondsmen." Such information wouldn't be available until after the license was granted, as there seemed "no doubt" the city clerk was following Mayor Boyd's directions. The result would be "poor and respectable dealers" unable to afford the license while "keepers of robber's roosts who can readily get the money" would get theirs, to the detriment of Omaha as a whole. The main purpose of the Slocumb Law would then be pointless.

The *Bee* continued on December 21, 1881, with an editorial titled "Mayor Boyd's Duty"; apparently, Omaha only had a dozen police officers for a city of forty thousand people. The newspaper continued its case:

"Omaha has a hard name abroad by reason of tolerating a disreputable class of disreputable dens, where bloody and murderous affrays and robberies are frequent." Even so, Omaha licensed "resorts where men and boys are decoyed by indecent shows and debauched and robbed." The *Bee* wondered why the mayor couldn't "suppress the St. Elmo with twelve policemen?" Why couldn't the mayor "close Dick Curry's and other dens" known for their "bloody frays" and "where gambling, prostitution and debauchery are carried on under the eyes of the police?" After all, "one policeman acting under orders of the mayor should be sufficient force to close any disorderly house," and if any "officer is resisted and it becomes a question of force," then Mayor Boyd should "call upon every law-abiding citizen to help him enforce law" and even ask the governor for military assistance. The pecking by the *Bee* continued on December 29, when the newspaper called it "a disgrace and an outrage that these infamous resorts have not been closed by the police" and claimed it "would be a greater outrage to have them licensed."

3
Slocumb

It was on New Year's Day 1882 when the Slocumb Law hit Omaha, and on January 2, the *Bee* described the Saturday night events after police visited the saloons with orders to close at midnight. Then, "for a wonder, the saloons obeyed," and at midnight, "everything was shut tight," while the next day the "front and back doors of saloons were ominously lonely and inaccessible"—contrary to all tradition. Only Turner Hall seemed willing to violate the Slocumb Law, as the Germans kept the beer flowing on Sunday. Otherwise, it was "Slocumb's Day" in the *Bee* on January 3, with officers distributing licenses to "fortunate applicants." The newspaper included a list of thirty-four legitimate liquor dealers and ten druggists allowed to sell alcohol, including Adalina Jahn, Herman Meyer, Amelia Thumb, Fred Metz, Henry Hornberger, Mrs. M. A. Higgins, J.G. Nugent & Co., John O'Connoll, John Svacina and F. Maus. It seemed "every applicant" was licensed, except a Mr. Treitscke and Dick Curry, who remained up for review.

By the end of January 1882, the *Bee* believed the Omaha police had "a soft thing" since Slocumb became the law. The amount of "Slocumbs, or plain drunks…[was] decidedly small." The newspaper also noted Officer McCune "was on the trail" of a notorious Twelfth Street prostitute who lured an unnamed man into her den of iniquity and got five dollars from him before she threw him out. The unnamed woman "kept shady," and the investigation proved "a dry haul." Also, John Roach, John Maguire and Michael Quinlan all pleaded guilty to "knife robbery" and claimed to be sixteen years old. None of the boys were that old, and they were sent to reform school.

These were the neighborhoods northeast of the courthouse that became the heart of Omaha's designated vice district. *Courtesy of Archives & Special Collections, Dr. C.C. and Mabel L. Criss Library, University of Nebraska at Omaha.*

Omaha was on the western itinerary of Oscar Wilde, who spoke at Boyd's Opera House at Fifteenth and Farnam on the evening of March 21, 1882. The *Bee* promoted the lecture and called Wilde "the father of so-called modern aestheticism." Wilde told his Omaha audience about the importance of beauty and art and left aboard the Union Pacific the next day for an engagement in San Francisco. More news that March included a report in the *Bee* that C.E. Westergard "swore out a warrant" against Samuel Rogers "for leasing a house to notorious prostitutes." The house in question was two rooms on the second floor of 108 North Twelfth Street—a "low dive" kept by Nellie Ross and Bella West. The *Bee* called that address "the center of what is known as 'Hell's half acre,' a place devoted almost entirely to the use of the lowest class of the demi-monde." The law said it had to be proved that Rogers "leased his property knowingly to notorious prostitutes." However, as Rogers was an "old resident" who owned lots of property, it seemed unlikely he wouldn't know the nature of his tenants' business or "the neighborhood in which they plied their nefarious traffic." The *Bee* pointed out the city's real dirty secret as "some of the oldest, wealthiest and most responsible citizens of Omaha" were renting property to prostitutes. "More than one greyhead" around Omaha would find themselves in court if everyone was "punished as they deserve."

The newspaper predicted "some racy developments" and a "revolution in the conduct and profits of the business of the nymphs du pave."

More progress appeared in the *Bee* at the end of May, with Omaha's "first step" to paving the city streets. Meanwhile, the marshal notified the women to leave Hell's Half Acre despite his belief that they would "scatter…about the city" to cause "many more complaints." The council still passed the motion to approve the "revised ordinances" against "'Disorderly Houses." This was not the last time Omaha struggled between segregating or dispersing vice across town. That action was just in time, as the American Woman Suffrage Association held its national convention in Omaha. The hotels were packed with cots set up in "anterooms, basements and parlors." Two days later, on September 15, the *Bee* reported Nebraska's "anti-prohibitionists" met in Omaha, where the number of saloons had declined "from 160 to 70." There would be even fewer if the law were "properly enforced." The next day, the *Bee* related that a farmer from Crete, Nebraska, named George Krug was stranded in the city after he was robbed on the Burlington train by the "Kansas City kid." The perpetrator was apprehended but escaped from Officer Timme, who fired three shots and missed. He was finally recaptured "near the old cracker factory" by Officer Timme with the assistance of a sheriff from an unnamed county. The outlaw had "passed the money to his partner…'Sly Bob'" by this time, though. The newspaper also reported a robbery aboard the train to Denver of $100 cash and a $1,000 check, "five drunks were run in by the police in the evening" and around midnight a "woman who was drunk and disorderly was hauled to the jail on a wheelbarrow."

There was "trickery all around" as Halloween 1882 approached, and the *Bee* reported that an unnamed woman who lived near Eighth and Douglas told police her daughter needed a doctor after she was "seriously" assaulted by "two of the Davis girls." They didn't have money for medical care, and she told "a harrowing tale." The sympathetic judge allowed the girl to see a doctor on the county's dime, and the mother's tears "melted the stony hearts" at the city clerk's office, which issued warrants for the Davis girls. The two Davis sisters both called it "nothing more than a hair pulling match all around," and the doctor sent by the county found out it was not the daughter but another woman with fever who really needed medical attention.

Omaha merited a mention the *New York Times* in January 1883—and not in a good way. The *Times* reported over 2,300 arrests in the city of 35,000 in 1882, including 660 for intoxication and 448 "inmates of houses of ill fame." Nebraska's metropolis then had 108 licensed saloons—or a saloon for every 325 people in the city. Downtown improvements continued, as Tenth and Douglas Streets were paved that year, and the *Bee* called for paving Harney and the rest of the streets between Ninth and Sixteenth. Something more familiar found its way into the *Bee* in early February with a "Hair Pulling Scene in the Halls of Justice." Judge Wright oversaw the case of Lizzie Reed, who sued Ralph Boone over fifty dollars she loaned him, along with "nursing him during sickness." As it was, the defense tried to make out Reed's reputation as less than credible, as "she had been the cause of considerable expense and suffering" for giving him the disease in the first place. Witnesses included Carrie Mullen, who been in court several times before "as a woman who believed in maintaining her rights 'vi et armis'" and had "once assaulted a sporting man" at Thirteenth and Douglas. She then threatened to "plaster" the crowd that gathered with "a handful of mud." The *Bee* dubbed Mullen "queen of the Omaha demi-monde, so far as beauty is concerned," but she was "as rich in temper as in good looks…[and] showed up in court this morning with a full hand."

During Reed's testimony, she claimed Mullen was "a woman of the town" and suggested Boone "had obtained his troublesome sickness from her." That was enough for Mullen, who "sprang from her chair like an enraged tigress and with one bound reached the witness." She took hold of Lizzie Reed by the hair and pulled off her wig. She then "went for the Reed woman like all possessed" until the constable and another man stepped in to stop it, afraid "the plaintiff in the case would be killed" right there in court. Mullen was hauled over to police court for disturbing the peace. She claimed Boone was "her intended husband," and Reed was "following him about, keeping him from work, and blackmailing him." The *Bee* quoted Mullen: "I ought to have whipped her long ago.…She shan't follow my man around and blackmail him." Her "eyes flashed and she set her lips as she spoke as if she could eat up a wagon load of women or men either." The case concluded with a verdict of thirty dollars for Reed.

Among myriad sensational news stories, on February 12, 1883, Lillie Woods—a sporting girl from Council Bluffs—appeared in the *Bee* after she visited Omaha and "got on a grand drunk." She paid a visit to Lottie Coombs's place on Capitol between Tenth and Eleventh and "got to smashing furniture" and "kicked a lighted lamp off the table, which exploded and set fire to the place." The fire was extinguished, and Woods then visited Barney Shannon's saloon in an attempt to "clean out the place, but was cleaned out herself." After that, she went back to Coombs's to tear it up some more—until two police officers ended her reign of destruction.

The *Bee* reported the two officers earned their pay "in getting Lillie to jail… [as] her foul language and screams drew a large crowd" along the way.

There was an account in the *Bee* on April 2, 1883, concerning a "stranger to the city" who visited a Tenth Street "house of ill-fame" on Friday, but "when he got ready to leave couldn't find his money." Naturally, he thought he had been "robbed and began blowing a police whistle." Of course, the stranger was arrested and then released from jail after paying the usual fine the next morning.

On May 12, the *Bee* reported the "new city marshal and his force" were on "active duty," but in early June, the newspaper still considered the number of thieves and con men in Omaha to be too high. One notorious swindler, Charles "Doc" Baggs, returned to Omaha with eight "companion spirits." Baggs was a "well known character in the days of Canada Bill" who earned a reputation "scarcely less notorious out west" with exploits from Deadwood to Denver and elsewhere.

"Depravity's Darlings" were back in the *Bee* in June 1883 with a "Raid on the Nymphs of Ninth Street." The newspaper claimed the "depths of depravity were stirred" with a Wednesday police raid "on the low dives" and

Boyd's Opera House—where Oscar Wilde lectured in 1882—stood at Fifteenth and Farnam until it burned down in the 1890s. *Courtesy of Archives & Special Collections, Dr. C.C. and Mabel L. Criss Library, University of Nebraska at Omaha.*

brothels along Ninth and Eleventh Streets. Most were hauled to jail after the resolution by the city council to clear out all dens of ill repute within two blocks of the Dodge Street School. The women arrested included nine from Ninth Street "of the lowest class" and five women from Eleventh Street a "shade more respectable." All made that night at the city jail "hideous with the blasphemy and obscenity" heard blocks away as the arrested "made the air blue with their oaths." One black prostitute "had a little boy when arrested" but managed to get him to a friend while a white prostitute was in jail with a "delicate and pretty featured boy." It was said the child wasn't hers, but he "sat up in the center of the cell, in the midst of the howling mob, with his eyes wide open" and little chance of sleep with the "hell that raged around him." The newspaper reasoned, "[C]hildren should be taken from the custody of such persons and provided with a home," but where that home might be wasn't addressed. The women all pleaded guilty, and a petition went around to have Anna Wilson's and John Wallace's on Douglas Street be "pulled the same as the rest." Wilson's and Wallace's were ignored by police, and the newspaper considered Wilson's "the most quiet and orderly place of its kind in the city." Still, both fell within the restricted area near the school. Someone who owned property on that block told the newspaper that they would file changes if the police failed to do their job.

However, the women were fighters according to the *Bee* on June 18, 1883, as the "effort to oust the lewd women" from the vicinity of the Dodge Street School was countered by "determined opposition." The eviction was also opposed by those "residents of the more aristocratic portions of the city with a storm of indignation." It was often said that "driving them off their old stamping ground…only scatters them broadcast throughout the city," as prostitutes appeared along Thirteenth, Sixteenth "and other streets, where they were never before tolerated" and where such women "offend the eyes of their more faultless sisters." It was said by the newspaper that other women "gather their skirts about them, like the Pharisee, and thank God that they are not like other women are." Either way, the thirteen women arrested as "inmates of houses of ill fame" all demanded a jury trial, and the case was continued for a week. The six members of the all-male jury were named in the newspaper, and the women hired four lawyers. There was also the possibility of putting the landlords—who rented to the women for "outrageous" sums—on trial. This was a common exploitation in Omaha: "One woman has paid as high as $75 per month for a house that was not worth $20."

The results of reform seemed a "sort of blood poisoning" in Omaha, and on June 23, the *Bee* called this the "natural result of too radical measures," with increased complaints from the "more respectable portions of the city" that prostitutes had moved into their neighborhoods. Two days later, the *Bee* reported the house on the southwest corner of Twelfth and Capitol—"so long known as Miss Jennie Dickinson's place"—had a "For Rent" sign. By June 27, the *Bee* was able to report that even Anna Wilson's brothel was "liable to be closed yet before the 'cruel war it over.'" Still, the newspaper predicted everything would go back to the same as before within two months. The newspaper anticipated that Mayor Chase's "declaration of war against the gamblers and prostitutes" would fail, and, as usual, the *Bee* was correct.

There was another "lively little squabble" on Twelfth Street near the old St. Elmo noted by the *Bee* on October 18. The fight broke out around midnight, and one Omaha police officer was hit over the head with a bottle. By December 1883, the "Dizzy Girls" were back in court to pay their monthly fines. It was the assessor who then went on the first of the month to list those "who are not employing legitimate means for obtaining a livelihood." They had until the December 10 to pay, and those who didn't were notified again before they were hauled in front of Judge Beneke and "either 'put up' or else are 'shut up.'"

The next Monday, the girls should have all paid, but few of them did. The *Bee* counted only 75 names for the month of December—a dubious number. With a sneer, the newspaper commented on "what a virtuous city Omaha must be." A marshal's report put the number of prostitutes closer

An 1889 view of Farnam Street with streetcars as the electric streetcar company's new bridge across the Missouri River from Council Bluffs took passengers right past Anna Wilson's. *Courtesy of Archives & Special Collections, Dr. C.C. and Mabel L. Criss Library, University of Nebraska at Omaha.*

to 300. The monthly fine was ten dollars for the "landladies," while the working girls were each fined six dollars. The *Bee* questioned why those 75 were singled out and another 225 "allowed to go right along and prosecute their unlawful business in the face and eyes of an outraged public."

How outraged Omaha was, was another matter, as the city's prostitutes could be found without much difficulty. The women were "doing business on some of our principal streets without any attempt at privacy or even decency." The *Bee* claimed authorities "simply wink and do not even hand in the names of such as they know to be prostitutes that they may be fined as the minority are." The newspaper believed "somebody gets something for thus withholding names of sirens in this city" but was unsure "whether it is the higher or lower officials." This author suggests the editor and publisher of the *Bee* knew very well where the unreported fines charged the other 225 prostitutes were distributed.

Another prostitute was in the *Bee* toward the end of December 1883 in an article concerning Georgia Sinclair's "Low Dive" near Twelfth and Capitol. The newspaper called it "one of the worst cases of depravity" seen in Omaha "for some time," as Sinclair was accused of "inducing" a fourteen-year-old and a fifteen-year-old "to have criminal intercourse with men." It was said both girls were from respectable families, and the "she-devil [Sinclair] enticed them into her hell hole [with] money and jewels." That's how she convinced them to let go "that which is of more value than all the gold of the Rocky Mountains…their virtue." The *Bee* considered Sinclair, who would "lead young girls into the very jaws of hell," was "unfit to even inhabit the infernal regions, and a man, no not a man, a beast who would accomplish the ruin of an innocent, especially under such circumstances, is too mean and low to be burned at the stake." Judge Beneke set Sinclair's bail at $2,000 for both charges. She couldn't pay and was sent to jail. If convicted, she faced a maximum of five years in the Nebraska penitentiary.

Omaha's nightlife was as wild as ever when the *Bee* profiled an "all-night hackman" in late December 1883. He told the newspaper he knew enough to "fill the *Bee* for several issues." "Yes," he said, "if that hack could talk, you would never lack for sensations." When asked if he would talk, the driver responded, "Of course I can, but I can't give anything away," as it would "be unprofessional as the lawyers say." He said his hack had "hauled home many a drunken man, who wouldn't have it known for the world" and "conveyed men and women, who claim to be respectable, to and from the road-houses." He had "carried eminently respectable men to places where they would not like to be seen," and sometimes women "who claim to be decent" still went "on a spree." There were gamblers who would rather pay for the ride than risk "being 'held up' and robbed" on their way home. The hackman told the *Bee* the job paid "very well" and "beats day work all to pieces." The best pay came from "confidential work," when his fare was "afraid of being given away." The hackman was paid up to ten dollars for a few hours, and "a $5 bill for an hour or two is a very common thing." The prices were paid by the "high-toned patrons, who know that a little extra pay will induce a man to keep a secret." He only received "ordinary pay" from "men who do everything open and above board, and do not care what the world says." It seemed those who paid the most "never ask me what I charge" but "simply pull out a five or ten dollar bill." They would say, "Stick that in your pocket. Don't give it away." To this, the hackman would respond, "Mum's the word."

In late December 1883, the *Bee* noted the Denver train was at the Omaha depot when a "lady passenger laid her purse upon the seat," and "she held her baby up to the window." While she was taking in the Omaha view, her purse was stolen. The next month, in January 1884, the *Bee* called a black prostitute named Belle Stewart "one of the slickest thieves in Omaha." She had "downed" a man for his "boodle" in the alley behind the Paxton hotel at Fourteenth and Farnam. It was a cold and snowy January that year when the sporting women paid for the funeral of Josie Moran. Moran "died at the corner" of Eleventh and Harney, but the *Bee* didn't reveal the cause. However, the cause of Owen Connelly's arrest that month was more obvious. Connelly was better known as "Whiskey Jack" and arrested for drunkenness on the complaint of his wife.

On January 14, the sensationalized story of a fourteen-year-old Iowa girl named Nellie Dubois hit the *Bee* after she left her home on an Iowa farm in favor of an Omaha brothel. The corruption of the country girl in the big city was familiar even then, and the newspaper considered this a "queer world" when "day after day, comes the story of children, brought up by respectable and pious parents, who have forsaken the paths of duty, virtue and right, to tread the downward road of misery, degradation and death." The newspaper considered it "all the more strange" that she would "voluntarily seek a life of shame and wickedness." It was her father, a farmer, who showed up in Omaha looking for his daughter. He found a police officer when he arrived and claimed his daughter left on New Year's Day with most of her clothes. He believed she'd been "induced to enter a certain house of ill-fame" in Omaha by a man in the military.

Dubois showed the police photographs of both his daughter and the noncommissioned officer who had been "corresponding with Nellie for some time" and visited her over the Christmas holiday. Nellie seemed "desperately

The neighborhood sure seem quiet in this 2016 view of Douglas looking east of Eleventh. *Author's collection.*

in love with him," but her parents were dubious, as they "saw certain indications" that he wasn't good for their daughter. Nellie's parents never "forbid him coming to the house" but still attempted to end the relationship. After their daughter left, they found a letter that "showed that the fears of the parents were not without foundation." The Iowa farmer and Omaha officer then visited "various bagnios" and finally found her in one. Nellie Dubois wouldn't leave until threatened with arrest. When they were leaving, the girl's lover showed up. Allegedly, it was the first time he had actually visited, and "when he met the father of the woman he would have ruined he was struck dumb." The Iowa farmer tried to attack the military man and would have killed him, but the officer intervened and escorted him and his daughter "away as quietly as possible." The officer took them to a hotel where they stayed until their return to Cedar Rapids. It was hoped that back on the farm, Nellie would "realize her narrow escape and behave herself in the future." She was described as "a pretty blonde, with pleasant features, vivacious ways and charming manners." Her father rewarded the unnamed officer a "golden eagle" coin, as "all concerned parted satisfied, except the man who had lured the girl from home."

4
Murder in a Variety Dive

Another abusive incident was reported by the *Bee* in early March 1884: Morris Vanan was found guilty of "beating one of the disorderly women of the town." Vanan was fined ten dollars and costs and sentenced to ten days in jail. Then, one Sunday evening, James Nugent was killed inside the old St. Elmo, then known as the Theatre Comique. The *Bee* revealed the "Bloody Sunday Work" at the "variety dive" as a reporter rushed to the scene to find 150 people milling around the building. The crowd was "all...excitement and rage," with women crying and men "engaged in swearing threats of vengeance." The dead man was inside on the floor, and except for the bullet hole in his head, "a casual observer would have said he was sleeping." The newspaper added that he was still holding "the stump of the cigar which he had been smoking," and the floor around him was "covered with the blood and brains."

There was an argument between Nugent and C.A. Sinclair over the vagaries of variety show business. Then "a stranger" exited the auditorium, saw the bickering and "started as if to strike Nugent a blow with all of his strength." A friend of Nugent named Frank O'Kinchel stepped between the the stranger and Nugent and said, "You son of a b——h! Don't touch him or I'll pummel the life out of you." Tom Price, a "gambler well known in this city as a bad man and a desperado," exited the auditorium and said to O'Kinchel, "You son of a b——h, I'll kill you" and drew "a revolver out of his hip pocket." O'Kinchel "jumped behind a man named Bob Russell" and over his shoulder watched Price approach "with his revolver cocked." All the while, proprietor Jack Nugent—James's brother—was still "sitting in a corner in front of the bar on a beer keg." Price walked up to Russell, jumped to one side and fired—missing O'Kinchel—hitting Nugent "directly in the forehead, penetrating the brain and causing instant death."

Price fired again and hit a man named Stout in the neck, but the shot wasn't fatal. Then, bartender John Keyes "seized a pistol, intending to shoot Price," but the gambler ran back through the auditorium—"revolver in hand, driving a great many spectators before him"—and escaped out the back door. He left behind "men shouting, wretched women weeping away their painted cheeks, police whistles blowing, and everybody in a state bordering on panic." To make matters worse, dogs found their way inside and "lapped up the blood and brains" that spread "in great pools upon the floor."

The wounded Stout was first taken to Schroeder & Becht's drugstore and then to jail to be held as a witness. Keyes the bartender, C.A. Sinclair, O'Kinchel and two other employees at the old St. Elmo were all arrested as either witnesses or for "complicity in the crime." The newspaper noted that Keyes was a former sheriff of Cherry County, Nebraska, who had "considerable newspaper notoriety." Sinclair claimed to be an actor and arrived in Omaha from Kansas City two weeks before. O'Kinchel was a painter and "a hanger-on for many weeks at several of the all-night resorts" in Omaha. As for Price, he had only been out of the Nebraska penitentiary for "four or five weeks" after serving four years for "safe blowing." Price had not been found when the newspaper went to press, and Sheriff Miller, Coroner Kent and Detective Neligh went to Council Bluffs to look for him. The murder weapon found in the auditorium was "an English bull dog self-cocking 44-caliber" with two empty chambers.

In addition to his brother's death, Jack Nugent would also have to deal with a complaint filed against him for being open on Sunday. The March 11 issue of the *Bee* noted that the same complaint had been filed against Tom Callan, C.S. Higgins and Fritz and Mina Wirth. The *Bee* also reported William Colver appeared in court "charged with creating a disturbance in a house of ill-repute" at Tenth and Harney. His case was continued in court in the familiar stall while the newspaper added that was "one of the hardest places in this city."

More details of James Nugent's murder were provided by the *Bee* while Price remained "at large," and many questioned around Omaha "who really did the killing." The county sheriff and coroner looked in "all the public places and bawdy houses" across the river—with assistance from the Council

Bluffs police—but couldn't find him. Price's description was requested from the Nebraska penitentiary and then "telegraphed to the sheriffs at Papillion, Fremont, and in all neighboring counties" along with a request to the governor wondering about the $200 reward Nebraska offered.

Nugent's business partner Harry Lucas said that Sunday he was selling tickets at the corner of the bar and told the *Bee* that he cashed a check for fifteen dollars for Stout. He claimed "Stout and Price entered the place together," and he called Jack Nugent over to tell him he didn't "like the looks of Price." Nugent called Lucas "an old granny" and said at that point, everything was all right. The shooting started fifteen minutes later.

The inquest was held at Drexel & Maul's undertaking parlor on Farnam. The six-member jury first heard from a Dr. Hyde, who "made a post mortem examination and found the bullet, flattened on two sides, in the back of the dead man's head." Dr. Hyde said "the pistol used in the shooting must have been held nearly on a level with Nugent's head." After that, the witnesses' testimony grew "so complicated that it was almost impossible to make anything out of it," including whether Keyes or Price killed Nugent. Keyes admitted to shooting twice "from behind the bar," and one bullet was found stuck in the wall across the room. It was that other bullet—"which left a heavy mark upon the bar"—that hadn't been found, unless, it was "the one that was taken from the brain of the dead man."

The *Bee* called Tom Price a "lawless fellow, and one who would stop at nothing" who had been "hanging around" Omaha for a few months claiming to be a gambler. Omaha gamblers denied that and told the newspaper Price "knew nothing at all about cards, and did not win or lose $5 a month." Instead, he was a "thoroughbred crook, and one of the hardest ones in the country" who would die "if he is cornered rather than be captured." It was said Price hid out "in a notorious house of prostitution" until a hack arrived to take him out of Omaha.

The *Bee* didn't have much good to say about Keyes either and called him "one of the hardest men in Nebraska." Keyes killed a county attorney in Texas, left and returned four years later to be acquitted. He then relocated to Nebraska and was elected sheriff of Cherry County. As sheriff, Keyes was "implicated in the murder of a man" and remained under indictment and out on bail. Afterward, Keyes returned to Texas, "committed some devilry and was obliged to skip out" and find his way as bartender at the old St. Elmo.

As for James Nugent, he was about twenty-two years old and a "hard drinker" who had been "on a protracted spree of several months." It was said Nugent told the coroner just a few weeks earlier that "he expected he would end up by someone's killing him." The coroner's jury agreed Nugent "came to his death by a pistol shot" but did not know who fired it. With that, the coroner "swore out warrants" for Price and Keyes on the charge of second-degree murder. When questioned, Keyes said he fired two shots and "did not know whether he killed Nugent or not," but from the "expression on his hardened feature one might infer that he didn't care."

In March, the *Bee* noted "Buffalo Bill" Cody and his wife were back in Omaha "from an extended theatrical tour." They planned several days in town "perfecting arrangements for the opening of his 'Wild West' show" and intended to buy a "large number of harnesses, saddles and other horse equipment." The opening of Cody's show for 1884 was planned for St. Louis on May 3. The newspaper also reported Omaha's saloonkeepers were still up to their old antics, and those accused of staying open Sunday nights showed up in court ready to have their cases continued. Fritz Wirth was particularly perturbed and "paced back and forth" in court, repeating, "Our mayor has gone back on us." When questioned, Wirth replied "Why…we, the saloon keepers elected him, and I worked awful hard for him, and now he has gone back on us." He claimed that if the saloons were closed up Sundays then so should the "barber shops, cigar store and drug stores, and the street railway company will have to quit running their cars."

More news concerning Tom Price appeared in the *Bee* on March 12. It seemed a few months earlier, he had been arrested in Council Bluffs with a friend for suspected involvement in a Denver robbery. Both were charged with "carrying concealed weapons, each being armed with a revolver." Price and his unnamed companion were finally released and all charges dropped. Price went to the Council Bluffs mayor to complain that they were arrested under a "malicious charge" and should get their guns back. The mayor agreed, and their revolvers were returned. Council Bluffs police believed that was the gun Price used to kill Nugent.

The *Bee* continued its crusade on March 13 against the "notorious variety dive" that remained "a resort for all sorts of outlaws" and had "done more to demoralize and deprave the young men of this city than any other so-called place of amusement." Nugent knew "many of the most dangerous characters" frequented his place—the bartender was an outright "desperado." The newspaper claimed "no malice," but the "violent death of his own brother" should convince Nugent such "dangerous resorts" should close. It was time for a "revolution in Omaha" and a "thorough cleaning out of the thugs, thieves and roughs." Otherwise, to end the "wave of lawlessness…[the] citizens will be compelled to organize in their own defense."

Two days later, the *Bee* reported the "notorious prostitute" Mamie Stitts caused a disturbance in a saloon at Eleventh and Capitol. She was taken to jail and pleaded not guilty the next morning, and her case was continued. Two weeks later, the *Bee* singled out prostitute Maggie Lindley on trial for intoxication. When her name was called, Lindley "stepped forward with a boldness and brazen-facedness which would put to shame the most hardened woman in shame," even though she was barely seventeen. She pleaded guilty and was fined ten dollars and costs. When she couldn't pay, Lindley "laughed and seemed to consider it a right good joke" as she was sent to jail.

It was in April 1884 when the *Bee* reported the new Omaha Stockyards Company was opening in the newly established city of South Omaha with space for eight thousand head of cattle. In time, the city of South Omaha—with its stockyards, packinghouses and immigrant neighborhoods—would be annexed, as Omaha became the world's largest livestock market. The sprawling stockyards cemented Omaha's status as a western cow town with drifting cowboys and refined cattlemen alike eager to see the sights. The Tuesday adventures of "two young fellows" appeared in the *Bee* on April 10 after they visited a certain Twelfth Street "concert saloon" and met black prostitutes Nell Austin

Fifteenth Street, the western fringe of Omaha's designated district of vice, in 1888. *Courtesy of Archives & Special Collections, Dr. C.C. and Mabel L. Criss Library, University of Nebraska at Omaha.*

and Clara Thomas. They all "drank some wine," but when they left, one man claimed he'd been robbed of eighteen dollars. Both women were arrested, while the newspaper clucked, "So long as men will visit such places and associate with such women they must expect to be robbed for that is the way such women gain a living." Once again, the *Bee* suggested no other potential employment opportunities. The newspaper also noted that the brothel of Maud Morris at 115 North Fifteenth Street was "pulled" by police. Morris and three unnamed women were hauled into jail, but the case was dismissed after they paid their six-dollar fines.

Also that April came the story in the *Bee* of an unnamed but "well known and respected citizen" of Omaha who had "the sad and disagreeable duty of searching for his fugitive daughter." It seemed the sixteen-year-old girl worked downtown and "became acquainted [with] and infatuated" by an older man. The father hired a detective who found his daughter "in a room" on North Twelfth Street "where she had been kept" since she left home. The young woman returned home with her father who filed a complaint charging the man with seduction.

Late that April, a funeral procession "nearly a half mile long" started on Douglas Street for gambler Dan Allen. The funeral at his home was crowded by a large "circle of his acquaintances and friends," who were all "anxious to pay a last tribute of respect." Allen's longtime companion Anna Wilson ensured he received a stone in Prospect Hill cemetery far more extravagant than the graves of most people in this book.

There was muck about the marshal thrown in the middle of May 1884, when the *Bee* reported Mayor Champion Chase insisted that complaints regarding Marshal Guthrie were to be put in writing, but there were already "several complaints about him in writing and in print" that Mayor Chase ignored. To the *Bee*, it seemed obvious that if the mayor really wanted proof of wrongdoing he only had to "look around" and questioned why "the low dives, where the crooks and sluggers congregate" were allowed to remain open. The *Bee* also wondered why "the marshal...failed to report between 200 and 300 'women of the town' to police court as he is duty bound?" and asked the question, "Who gets the money which these abandoned women pay from time to time to escape arrest?" The *Bee* noted that "perhaps the mayor wants these blackmailed women to make complaint in writing" and further questioned how it was "the most inoffensive persons are arrested and lodged in jail as vagrants, while cut-throats, sluggers, thieves, confidence men, and other crooks are allowed to run at large?"

One crook was the notorious Sadie McBride, who had been arrested for robbery, according to the *Bee* of May 15. After McBride "enticed a young man named Miller into her den," she "struck him, knocking him down." Then she "threatened to kill him if he did not give up his money," and Miller handed over what amounted to three dollars before he fled her domicile.

At the end of May, the *Bee* buzzed with the knowledge that the police regularly visited the "saloons and gambling houses at all hours of the day and night," where they met and mingled "with the crooks, roughs and roustabouts." The newspaper claimed the "vilest dens" were allowed to "run night and day unmolested," with Omaha under a "reign of lawlessness" worse than Cheyenne, Deadwood or Leadville. All blame was directed at Marshal Guthrie and claimed the recent raid on the red-light district was a "blackmailing job," as brothel owners paid $250 to be "let alone" and funds were "divided among certain officials." While that "system of bleeding and blackmailing" had been going on in Omaha for a long time, it remained a "fraud and disgrace" and an "outrage upon the victims." Marshal Guthrie reported only forty to sixty prostitutes to the police court, but there were "fully three times as many known to the police." The newspaper wondered if these women were allowed to go free and what happened to the fines.

Rosewater's *Bee* readily printed Marshal Guthrie's assertions that "all the unfavorable insinuations…were false and malicious." The *Bee* chose to take the marshal at his word and singled out Nugent's "disorderly house" and longtime "resort of the lawless element." It was at the old St. Elmo where "men have been robbed, beaten and even murdered," and Marshal Guthrie knew all about it. That was after many complaints from "respectable men and women, whose sons have been led into immoral habits and a bad life" due to the St. Elmo. The *Bee* declared Marshal Guthrie "either shirked his duty" or was involved with these dangerous businesses.

John Keyes came back to Omaha from Valentine, Nebraska, at the end of May to face charges in the murder of James Nugent. That was after the grand jury out in Cherry County didn't indict him for murder. It seemed generally accepted that Keyes unintentionally fired the fatal shot, but the case against him soon fell apart in court.

At the end of May, the *Bee* again brought up the fact that the Dodge Street School remained "surrounded by the lowest houses of prostitution and the vilest dives and dens in the city." The newspaper believed everything would "be brought to the attention of the grand jury," as something had to be done to clean up Hell's Half Acre.

One month later, on June 30, the *Bee* announced a raid on the women of the town, with forty-eight prostitutes rounded up along with twenty male patrons. The newspaper considered them a bad lot. The next morning at court, almost twenty of them were fined the usual five dollars and costs. They were described as "very tough-looking" but "homely as a hedge-fence and shabbily dressed," as though they had "been run through a threshing machine." They were subjected to the stares from a crowd of spectators as they were seated and waited for their names to be called.

Prostitute Lou Prince got a brief mention in the *Bee* on July 15 after she "attempted to commit suicide on Saturday by taking morphine." However, a "good big emetic saved her from crossing the dark river." She died all the same in Lou Scott's house on Dodge near Ninth Street, where her funeral was held at the end of July. The "disorderly women of Omaha" raised the money to bury her "in a good coffin and in a grave lot" instead of Potter's Field. The funeral procession included fifteen carriages and a sermon at the grave site by Reverend Harris. That issue also gave news of Marshal Cummings's orders to Ed Hunter, Tom Callan, Rasmus Rasmussen, Charles Schrote, August Utoff & Company and Mrs. H. McCoy, who were delinquent in paying the second installment of their liquor licenses and notified to close or face arrest. As for Omaha's "war on gamblers," the marshal ordered gambling places closed within twenty-four hours—with little effect—and "swore out complaints" against C.S. Higgins, Hiram Kennedy, Seth C. Baldwin, Jack Morrison, Goodly Brucker, William Soderstrum, Jack Woods and their dealers and charged them with being gamblers.

The July 1884 accounting of police court appeared in the *Bee* early the next month. Of the 451 cases, 101 were for prostitution and 2 cases of "renting houses to prostitutes." Items from court reported in that issue included Adam Bleedenbower, who was arrested at the old St. Elmo "for refusing to pay $3 for a swallow of wine." It seemed "one of the girls bulldozed out of him" the bottle of the wine, but no one was there to testify against him so he was released. The "notorious" Clara Thomas wasn't as lucky; she was fined ten dollars and costs for fighting. The fight between Thomas and Belle Sanford was "more serious than supposed," as Sanford received a fractured skull and a broken left arm.

Times remained wild. In August 1884, the *Bee* reported two men—"one of them a prominent saloon-keeper in this city"—who were racing their horses one Sunday down Sixteenth Street. They crossed Dodge Street with their horses running "not far from a three-minute" mile. The newspaper reminded readers it had only been a fortnight since a woman was run over on Sixteenth Street and predicted that someone would be killed unless such actions were stopped.

At the end of August, "complaints in regard to disorderly houses…[became] louder and louder…pouring in from all parts of the city," as many prostitutes relocated to residential neighborhoods. That included a brothel located "within a stone's throw" of the First Methodist Church, one on Capitol Avenue between Fifteenth and Sixteenth Streets and another one, possibly two, as far west as Seventeenth Street between Harney and Howard. There was another "notorious house" on Fourteenth Street between Jackson and Jones that caused a "loud protest" from the respectable citizens who lived nearby and another on Jackson between Thirteenth and Fourteenth Streets. And, of course, there were still two brothels near the Dodge Street School supposedly "owned by a prominent city official," who rented to "some of the very lowest prostitutes." It wasn't just the brothels themselves but the "manner in which the prostitutes conduct[ed] themselves upon the streets" and "flaunt[ed] their shame in the faces of respectable women and fairly crowd[ed] them from the sidewalk into the street." The prostitutes were said to "drive through the streets in open carriages at breakneck speed apparently defying all law and order...every day and night in Omaha."

The same tricks played out at the old St. Elmo with "another case of robbery" in the *Bee*. That was after two drugstore clerks paid a visit to Omaha's storied variety theater and "were bulldozed into paying for a bottle of wine much against their will." It seemed "Bill Armour was there with his club," and it was "pay or go to jail." The two clerks paid.

There was "a large crowd of idlers" reported at Omaha Police Court on October 2 after news went out that Ella Mitchell's brothel was raided." A "one legged tailor" named A. Lindholm was charged with intoxication and "beat about the bush considerably" before pleading guilty. He was fined five dollars and costs, as were two other men charged with the same offense. A prostitute named Mamie Stilts was also charged with intoxication, pleaded guilty and fined ten dollars and costs. Flora Smith, Ettie Seaman, Clara Thomas, Blanche Carter, Alice Walters and Mollie Price were each fined five dollars and costs as ladies of the night.

In November 1884, the *Bee* reported another modernization: the city planned to equip policemen who patrolled downtown at night with lanterns. There was also a young man who had a good job and "caught his wife, a young woman noted in Omaha for her beauty, in the society of one of the disorderly women of the town." The typically sober man went over to Council Bluffs to get drunk and returned to Omaha the next day announcing his intentions to get a divorce.

A dozen disorderly women made their way into the *Bee* on November 18 after they failed to pay the first of the month fee. All were released after paying $7.55. The next day's issue listed only one woman charged as "an inmate of a house of prostitution," and she was released after paying "the usual." On November 25, the *Bee* reported Omaha had earned $721.15 from "fines and costs collected from gamblers and prostitutes" during the previous August. Two days later, on November 27, came another sad case, with the death Anna Pickard "in a tumbled tenement house" near Ninth and Dodge. The newspaper called her a "disorderly woman" whose corpse "was properly cared for and the stove removed from the room." Her intoxicated husband returned and insisted the stove be put back. After "considerable time and argument," the man was convinced his wife's "corpse would keep better without a fire." Flora Benson, Martin Connelly and an unnamed soldier sat up "watching the body during the night." They got drunk, and a fight broke out in which the soldier used a razor to cut Connelly's jaw "to the bone." When police arrived, "the body was found taken from its bed and lying partly naked on the floor." The police sent for an undertaker and arrested Benson and Connelly. The police did not find the soldier. Soon after, on December 4, the *Bee* reported on a suicide: the morphine overdose of eighteen-year-old Maud Bramer. She had been fired from Carrie Mullen's Capitol Avenue brothel, and her real name was Esther Singleton.

By December 1884, the *Bee* claimed Omaha remained "infested with thieves, burglars and thugs" and almost hated to admit it was "the rendezvous" for "as hard a gang as ever 'scuttled ship or cut a throat.'" There were all sorts of criminals "from the assassin down to the miserable sneak thief" with officials supposedly powerless. If it were only thieves and burglars, the situation wouldn't be so bad, but "so desperate are the criminals" who holed up in Omaha that winter that violent deeds were common.

5
The Dark Idol

The Omaha Belt Line railroad opened its suburban loop around the city in 1885, and the *Bee* reported the New Year was kicked off with "snow in large quantities...blown hither and thither by a strong wind." There were "many ears and noses...touched by the frost," among gambler J.C. Newton's frozen fingers. Newton was found by police in a vacant lot on Ninth between Dodge and Douglas Streets while lying "flat on his back and about half covered over with snow." He was taken to jail, where "his hands were found to be badly frozen" and so "white with frost and badly swollen" as to look like deer antlers. The jailer set about to "thaw the man's hands" with snow and then soaked them in cold water. The gambler's "hands were then rubbed until the blood began to circulate, after which sweet oil was applied in liberal quantities." Newton "suffered greatly" after his hands thawed, as they were swollen with "large water blisters." He was later taken to St. Joseph's hospital. The newspaper also reported Omaha's accumulated 342 crimes for December 1884, with 79 arrests each for intoxication and prostitution.

At the end of January 1885, the *Bee* reported that eight tramps walked into a saloon at Tenth and Jones and demanded whiskey. When denied, one tramp "put his hand in his hip pocket in a threatening manner," but when the bartender reached for his revolver, the tramps "beat a hasty retreat." The newspaper also described the latest from the "Dead Beat" Buckingham at the old St. Elmo, still "run in a disgraceful manner," as it wouldn't pay for anything it didn't have to. The theater owed money for advertising "to nearly every paper in this city" and was even unwilling to pay the help. Maud Clifford and Lillie Morris worked for four weeks before they went to the *Bee* to air their "grievances." The two were hired via telegraph and had "no idea of the kind of a place that was being run" in Omaha. They arrived almost broke and "went to work" for a promised twenty-five dollars weekly. Instead, they had only been paid ten dollars each for the past four weeks and had pawned their belongings to survive. The two women said they were "used to playing in nice houses and going home as soon as their work was finished." At the old St. Elmo, they were required to remain until three o'clock in the morning "in the wine room" to accompany the "gang of prizefighters and thugs." The Saturday night dances kept going until seven o'clock the next morning and attracted the "lowest class of prostitutes" and "more vile and low-lived hurrahs have never been witnessed in Omaha." When the two woman were due to leave for an engagement at the Palace Theatre in St. Louis and asked for their pay, they "were met with the most vile and profane language." Nugent wouldn't pay them "a single cent." At the same time, the marshal notified owners of the old St. Elmo that it would be closed unless the business's delinquent liquor license was paid. The *Bee* moralized a "greater portion of Omaha's citizens sincerely hope that it will not be paid" and that the infamous "sink hole of iniquity" would close forever and its "owners driven from the city" for good.

It seemed Omaha even had a juvenile school for robbery. Twelve-year-old Dan Thompson was in court "charged with stealing a book," but the boy claimed Will Miller was the thief and intended to sell it to "a Mrs. Bull" on Tenth Street. It seemed this Mrs. Bull "bought such things and even sends out small boys to steal for her, paying them a premium upon all they bring in." The *Bee* declared it was "high time that the city be rid of this school for crime" and Mrs. Bull run out of Omaha for good. Thompson had twenty cents to his name but spent the sum playing pool at O'Connell's on Tenth Street. This revelation left the judge "thunderstruck" to discover "boys only twelve years old were allowed to play pool." That seemed "about the only class of custom this man O'Connell has and he has small stools made for the little boys so that they can reach up to the table to make a shot." A petition was promptly filed against O'Connell "for allowing minors to play in his place" and Thompson was slated for reform school.

Concerning itself with the upcoming elections, the *Bee* suggested a Mr. Caulfield as Third Ward candidate for city council, as not "every councilman from the Third Ward" had to be a bartender. By early April, all Omaha's gamblers were "stirred up" over the elections, as the newspaper pounced on anything to promote its own candidate. The Omaha gambling houses then included Morrison's, Baldwin & Kennedy's above Clark's saloon, Wood's on Douglas between Twelfth and Thirteenth, Higgins's on Douglas and Soderstrom's right on Farnam. All were known as "square games," and the *Bee* compared the era under Mayor Boyd with "ten to one more gambling going on than ever before or since." That was debatable, but the *Bee* rarely let facts interrupt its message. The newspaper recalled the days of 1882, when "young Donnelly" ran a "skin game" on Twelfth Street between Farnam and Douglas and singled out keno as "something never heard of in Omaha, except in the very early days when the city made no pretension to being well governed." There were also "innumerable poker rooms," and the *Bee* claimed it was "pretty well known" Mayor Boyd "does not object to a little game of draw, and in fact rather likes it." However, Mayor Murphy was not that sort of man. As for the old St. Elmo, the paper and others were pleased to note the odious establishment would have its license revoked. Nugent filed his application and paid $100 but never followed through with the remaining provisions. James McVey then "garnished" the $100 and left Nugent unable to sell liquor. Many wondered why the city marshal didn't close up the place.

In mid-April 1885, the *Bee* brought up the "dark idol" of opium after rumors that the marshal would "close up the opium joints" before expected action by city officials. The newspaper predicted "total suppression," as "of all the mysterious and terrible features of criminal life in Omaha," nothing was as mysterious as the opium dens hidden behind "a dark veil of almost impenetrable secrecy." Omaha's "confirmed opium-eaters" were "forever doomed" by the drug. Four joints singled out included one on Twelfth Street next to the old St. Elmo. The others were located on the west side of Tenth Street between Douglas and Dodge, on the north side of Harney between Eleventh and Twelfth and at Thirteenth and Dodge. All these joints were "run in connection with Chinese laundries," with rooms "of the plainest character possible" and "not the slightest attempt at anything sumptuous." The newspaper thought that the norm in "every opium joint from New York to San Francisco"—except for the private setups of the wealthy opium eaters.

Admittance was almost impossible, and "any curiosity seeker…[found] the doors literally and figuratively closed." The Chinese laundrymen show a "painful ignorance of any such thing as opium-smoking" and would likely order inquisitive guests out "in pigeon [*sic*] English." A *Bee* reporter only gained access to a joint from someone "initiated into the mysteries of the 'divine' drug." The entrance was right through the laundry in the front of the building where the Chinese immigrants were hard at work. Then he went out a "back entrance and up a rickety flight of stairs into a back room" where opium was sold and smoked. The "walls are covered with small bunks or beds, one above another," and the newspaper detailed the opium pipe and process of smoking "the opium or 'hop' as the Chinamen call it." Any description of the "opium smoker's heaven is vain…supremest ecstasy" followed by a "terrible depression of spirits, by a racking and torture of the physical frame, by a fall into the deaths of despair" until more opium was smoked.

More details came from a gentleman who knew "every phase of the vice" and told the newspaper "many people imagine…the only people who use opium are the members of the 'lower strata,' gamblers and all that class of people." True, "the vice is largely confined to these classes, it is by no means absolutely so.…I could give you the names of a number of people right here in this city, regarded as respectable, who are confirmed opium smokers." The man continued the "cost of a smoke" was twenty-five cents for every "pill of 'hop' or opium" and a "confirmed opium smoker" could smoke up to a one hundred pills in a night. The informant also noted older opium pipes increased in value, with antique apparatus worth forty to fifty dollars. There was "some sort of secret sign among the hop smokers" that identified them, but otherwise the dens were "strictly guarded and closed against all outsiders."

The *Bee* finally announced on April 22 that the Buckingham—the old St. Elmo—was closed and followed with a dare to authorities to "see that it stays closed." It wasn't the murders or fights or scams or prostitutes but instead Nugent's poor business practices that brought the curtain down. While surely Nugent could find the funds to carry on, the newspaper suggested the days of such places were over. Instead, "high-priced theatres, operas, circuses, and all exhibitions" were Omaha's future sources of entertainment.

Without the old St. Elmo to hold up for all to see, the *Bee* found a new crusade: Omaha must "throw out the opium." Mayor Boyd planned to shut down the opium joints and perhaps even force saloons to close at midnight and on Sundays. The first details of the opium crackdown came to light on May 2, after eighteen Chinese were charged "for the first time in the history of the city" with "keeping opium joints, or being inmates thereof." Often dubbed "celestials" by the Western press, all the Chinese had lawyers and got their cases continued. About half made bail, and the rest sat in jail.

The Temperance Union moved into the old St. Elmo, and the *Bee* printed "An Appeal" at the end of May. The newspaper noted the "Herculean task of redeeming that notorious place" and asked for aid from "churches and moral people of Omaha" to transform "the theatre into a temple for gospel temperance work, the saloon into a lunch room, and the wine room into a reading room." There were also "two sick rooms above," and it was hoped the churches would provide beds and linens. The organizers planned this to be "a working girls' home, where poorly paid girls can find cheap board" and where "penniless girls" could live until they found a job. The Temperance Union requested donations of money along with

wall paper and paint, carpets, one-half dozen tables, 300 chairs for auditorium, silver knives, forks and spoons, restaurant dishes, napkins and towels, oil cloth for covering tables, pictures, mottoes, vases, plants, literature, piano or organ, water coolers, refrigerators, kitchen furniture complete, including gasoline stove and cooking utensils, door and window screens.

The transformation was trumpeted by the *Bee* in mid-June 1885 as the newspaper recounted the location's history as the "vilest of the vile—the very center of that portion of town where are to be found all the lowest elements of life." The St. Elmo was "one of the lowest variety dens in the west," and conditions were not improved by changing its name to the Theatre Comique and then the Buckingham.

By August 1885, the *Bee* had nothing but praise for the Temperance Union's lunch room at the old St. Elmo. That was in spite of "many petty annoyances" that included "mud and filth of all kinds" thrown in the "ice-water barrel" that sat out front, as "some of the people in the neighborhood are in the habit of emptying it either by carrying off the water for their own use, or by leaving the faucet 'turned on,' and allowing the water to run out." The Temperance Union also complained of "petty thefts and depredations," and some had sought to stop them from selling buttermilk. They believed "parties in the neighborhood" wanted "exclusive right" to sell buttermilk, but it was more likely just its neighbors causing trouble.

The fall of 1885 seemed full of suicide. On October 1, the *Bee* reported that an infamous black prostitute named Belle Sanford had attempted to take her own life. She lived on Eleventh Street and overdosed on laudanum, an opium derivative. When discovered, Sanford "was unconscious and in spasms," but a Dr. Ricketts revived her. The cause seemed to be "one of the 'white trash,' with whom she had become infatuated, who yesterday went off with another colored lady." That "nearly broke Belle's heart and she concluded to die." Another attempted suicide was Rose Davis, who lived above Neber's saloon at Thirteenth and Harney. Davis swallowed a bottle of hensbane, and a Dr. Swetnam was summoned to save her. His success brought "a stream of vituperative abuse" from Davis, who attempted to run the doctor and his attendant out of her room. The newspaper called Davis George Schrieber's mistress and reported that "she was sick, disgusted, and tired of life." The *Bee* agreed with the adage that everything happens in threes on October 5 during an inquest into the death of J.D. Bosnell. He killed himself one Friday night at the bagnio of Madam Leepe. The coroner received a telegram from Bosnell's brother-in-law in Illinois with instructions to bury him in Omaha.

The Temperance Union's work in the old St. Elmo was again profiled by the *Bee* in the middle of December. The once notorious saloon, theater and brothel was a thing of the past. The Temperance Union rented the fourteen rooms for $75 a month, and over $600 was spent to transform the wine room into an "attractive reading room" and turn the saloon into a restaurant. In the six months since the Temperance Union took over, there were eighty-eight meetings and 234 "gratuitous meals" given out. Sometimes volunteers resorted to makeshift beds on the floor along with the five beds "always ready for the homeless." Sometimes, "bedding is not always equal to the need," and nothing much has changed in that regard.

The old St. Elmo became a refuge for some, including a seventeen-year-old girl on her way to the West who was "taken sick at Chicago" and spent all her money. She was then "passed on to Omaha," where she was cared for by the Temperance Union "until a pass was secured." There was also a young woman with a child who "received the care and protection needed during several weeks of sickness" along with a sixteen-year-old girl "saved from the snares laid to her ruin by two designing knaves." There were an equal number of young men who needed help, and some of them—young and old—admitted they had attended the "old variety theater" but now attended the "gospel meetings." A ladies' prayer meeting was every Thursday, and on Sundays, the once notorious theater hosted English classes for Chinese immigrants, who were also instructed in the Scriptures and learned gospel songs. Still, finding help proved hard, as the "harvest is truly great, but the laborers are few." The lunch room was "only paying its running expenses" and was intended for "many young men who might go to unsafe places for warmth, food and drink."

Another Douglas Street "house of bad character" was raided by police, according to the *Bee* on December 24. The landlady, May Wallace, was fined twenty dollars and costs, while Mattie Lee and Bertie Simpson were both fined three dollars and costs. A "male inmate" named Howard Smith was fined five dollars and costs. That issue also offered a "mysterious sensation" after a "big, fat man rushed down the platform of the Union Pacific depot" and jumped aboard the train to Lincoln as it was preparing to leave the station. The man was "wild with excitement and sweating with exertion" and his words "profanely Dutch" as he sprinted through the depot to jump aboard. He ran through the first passenger car while "giving the occupants one wildly sweeping glance." When he entered the second car, a "good-looking young woman, seated in a middle section," stood up and screamed. The fat man said something, laid hold of her and "before the passengers were aware" dragged the young woman off the train and pushed her through the depot toward the Tenth Street exit.

Outside, the man then shoved the woman into a waiting hack that "was whipped away" by the driver. Before the sensation at the depot was over, the hack came back "at a gallop," and the "young woman sprang out alone with her hair disheveled as though she had passed through a struggle and face blanched in evident fear." The woman ran back through the depot and jumped aboard the Lincoln train as the "wheels were already moving." The newspaper thought the story must be a "first-class sensation," but failed to find out what really happened.

Another attempt to reign in the saloons was made in mid-February 1886 with a second reading of the ordinance that, according to the *Bee*, allowed "them to run all night" but close on Sundays. It was noted that "the general sentiment of the people was in favor of leaving well enough alone." The council courageously tabled the issue by a unanimous vote. There remained trouble aplenty with a "Stabbing Affray" at a "Colored Gambling Dive" reported by the *Bee*. The dive in question was above Peter King's saloon at Eleventh and Capitol, and several black men were shooting craps at Peter Green's dice game. Among the players was John Dixson, better known as "Stuttering John," who had been unruly all night until Green finally kicked him out of the game. When Dixson refused, Green tried to physically remove him, but Dixson pulled out a knife and stabbed Green repeatedly. Needless to say, this "took the other men in the room by surprise," and Dixson took the opportunity to run downstairs and out into the street—right into the arms of Officer Donovan. The officer "heard the racket" and was waiting. Stuttering John was taken to the police station and charged with "stabbing with intent to kill." Green's friends took him to the police station, where his wounds were treated and he was held as a witness.

On May 7, the *Bee* reported another attempt to run out the Cyprians when one Omaha councilman brought attention "to the disorderly row of dens" on the north side of Capitol Avenue between Ninth and Tenth Streets. The area was home to "mostly colored prostitutes," and the council ordered the marshal to tell them to relocate. Some left, but "others were refused houses wherever they applied." Among those affected were a black woman named Maud Miller and her seven employees: Hattie Payne, Mary Wilson, Maggie Cooper, Ida Jones, Bell Smith, Fannie Price and Belle Sanford. Their fate under the new provisions was uncertain, as they always paid the city in a timely fashion.

Some folks were luckier than others, and on September 4, the *Bee* related one example. It seemed a "decidedly dilapidated fellow" begged a meal from an Omaha restaurant owner who, "contrary to custom…did not throw the man bodily out of the place." After eating his free meal, the man approached the restaurant owner and told him that he wished to be staked in a game of faro. The restaurant owner agreed to put up $0.50, and "within less than five minutes the fellow was seated at a faro table" in an Omaha gambling hall and "won from the start." Every draw of the cards "threw gold and silver into his pile," and he left the game the next morning "nearly $1,300 ahead." The gambler then spent $200.00 on "treating the large crowd" that had watched him all night. After that the unnamed gambler paid back his debt to the restaurant owner, he "walked away with over $1,000 in his pockets."

Not as lucky were "two cow-boys from the wild west on their way east" who passed through Omaha in late November. They were the victims of "sneak thieves" one Sunday night "at a cheap lodging house." When they went to bed, they both put their "vests, containing their watches and money" underneath their pillows and were robbed all the same. One cowboy lost a watch and $4.50, but the thieves missed the $50.00 "in another pocket." The other lost $20.00 but kept his "fine gold watch." The two went to the police but "could give no clue" as to who robbed them.

Another husband looking for his wife made his way into the *Bee* at the end of December 1886 with the story of a "sad-eyed man from Lincoln" who found his "erring wife" in an Omaha brothel. He gave the name Charles Johnson when he approached the police for help in finding his wife, "who had deserted him and was supposed to be in Omaha." This man Johnson said he was a confectioner in Nebraska's capital city and they had a one-year-old child. Then, two weeks before, his wife "showed signs of being discontented with her rather humble lot" and then said she would leave him. Johnson ignored her, but last week "he went home from his work and found his wife had gone away and left their baby without a word." He heard she was in Omaha with "evil associations" and so came to the state's metropolis. Johnson provided "an accurate description of the woman," and with the help of an officer, Mrs. Johnson was found at a house on Fourteenth Street kept by Big Stella Young.

Johnson entered Big Stella's to find his missing wife dressed up "in the most approved style of the beauties of the lower order." The man "gazed at her a moment" and then took her into his arms and started to cry. His wife proved "very penitent" at first and "asked for her baby and forgiveness" and "promised to return with her husband to the home she had deserted and disgraced." However, while she was packing up her belongings, "the other inmates of the place persuaded her to change her mind." That's when she announced the "chilling information that she had decided to stay where she was." It seemed Johnson wasn't "very good to her at her home anyway, and she guessed, on the whole, she wouldn't take any stock in his promises of reform…[and] would let him go home alone." The Lincoln confectioner was "crushed…completely" and left only after the officer refused to "help him remove the woman by force." It was said he would return to Lincoln alone if he couldn't convince his wife go back home with him.

The city's industrial character continued to develop in 1887 with construction of the Bemis Bag Company building at Eleventh and Jones Streets, now the home of the Bemis Center for Contemporary Arts. The Broatch Building, which still stands at 1209 Harney Street, was expanded to four stories that year, and the famed Diamond gambling house at 1313 Douglas Street was opened by gamblers Charles Bibbins, Blanche Kennedy, James Morrison and Charles White. The Diamond was the mainstay for high-rollers until it closed in 1893.

There were 221 women listed as Omaha prostitutes in the *Bee* in February 1887, and late the next month, the newspaper claimed the "Dives Must Go" from Capitol between Ninth and Tenth Streets. Omaha's city council told the marshal to "go ahead and have the houses vacated." This disposal of "very bad rubbish" was greeted with joy by the more respectable residents. At the same time, "decent people on neighboring streets" were "filled with fear and trembling," as the wholesale running out would just send such pleasure houses to their neighborhoods.

Then there was also "wealthy cattleman" R.W. Hyde from Malvern, Iowa, who took in what Omaha offered one Sunday night. He was "drugged and robbed" after visiting saloons at Twelfth and Douglas and another a block east. Hyde woke up the next morning "lying very near a steep cliff or bluff by Boyd's packing house," and if he had rolled over, the motion would have propelled him over the cliff to die on the railroad tracks below. He also lost "$12,000 in notes, drafts and checks" along with $50 in cash and his gold watch and chain, valued at $150. He included "two hackmen" in his tale of woe and returned to Iowa to stop payments at his bank.

The persistence of opium in Omaha continued, and at the end of March 1887, the *Bee* singled out the city's "most notorious den," on Twelfth Street between Douglas and Farnam. That's where "notorious hop fiends" visited "all hours of the day and night." The neighbors complained about the persistent smell, "a sickly, oppressive odor" outside the den, which was patronized by gamblers and loose women. Omaha's other opium dens were on Sixteenth, Harney and Tenth, where "the opium smoker can enjoy a quiet 'siesta' at 25 or 50 cents a pipe." One police officer told the newspaper "this evil has grown so in Omaha" that all the Chinese laundries offered their own opium services.

On April Fool's Day 1887, the *Bee* reported Nellie Scott had committed suicide around eleven o'clock in the morning the day before with an overdose of morphine. Twenty-two-year-old Scott was an "inmate of the bagnio" at 1311 Jones Street and "occupied a room in the house where she died" for about three weeks. She'd only been in Omaha twice that long. It was said her mother lived in Beloit, Kansas, and she had two brothers in Van Meter, Iowa. The landlady of the Jones Street brothel said she had a husband who "left her a day or two ago," and that's why she killed herself. The inquest ruled it a suicide, and Scott's body was taken by an undertaker, as "friends of the dead girl have not been heard from." Many people went to see the body, "with a morbid curiosity for such spectacles," including the newspaper, which printed the "dead girl had coarse, irregular features, which were not especially attractive."

Later that same month, on April 22, the *Bee* reported a "lively day for the frail females," with police raids on a "half dozen of the places of notorious repute," with papers served on another twenty-one brothels. The landladies were all fined twenty dollars and costs, with ten dollars and costs each for the women. By noon, fifteen of the twenty-one brothels paid a visit to police headquarters and paid up. There were also five men taken in during the raid, and they were each fined twenty dollars and costs. The *Bee* noted the names of the men "were not obtainable, and right here is an opportunity." The newspaper called on either the mayor or judge to "require that every man's name as arrested be placed upon the docket so that they could be published in company with all other offenders, a way would be opened for some genuine reform." Omaha's "John Doe business" was too much, and "if prominent names were listed in company with poor fellows who cannot escape publicity, society would see every once in a while a star actor up in police court."

The Temperance Union left the old St. Elmo in May 1887, and by early June, the *Bee* noted their relocation to a German church in the 1200 block of Dodge Street. That issue also recounted how John Wallace, "who runs a dive" on the corner of Ninth and Douglas, was arrested with his wife and Jessie Moore. They were all charged with "stealing a gold ring from a girl visitor to the joint." There was also a notice from Mayor Broatch concerning action by the Nebraska legislature to close up the gambling halls. The *Bee* expected "baseball combinations" sold at the Exchange pool hall would be considered gambling under the new law and ended.

Belle Sanford was back in the *Bee* on September 20 as "keeper of a house of fame" after police were called to Eleventh and Capitol. Sanford was hauled in, and when she got out of the wagon at the police station, "she carried a babe" and was followed by "a little four-year-old girl." Then from "the floor of the wagon was taken the insensible and bleeding form of a man" who had apparently "visited the dive run by Belle" and had been thrown out of Belle's not long before her arrest. The man "was quite drunk and strongly objected" to getting thrown out, and Sanford met "those objections" with "a big club" and "beat him about the head in a terrible manner." He was unconscious when Officer Brady picked him up, and a doctor attended to him at the police station. Due to the severity of his injuries and state of intoxication, his name remained unknown.

Another beating in the *Bee* in late October 1887 concerned the arrest of Jacob Swartz, known as "Dutch Jake." He was proprietor of the bawdy house near the corner of Eleventh and Capitol and arrested for beating Edward Smith with a cane. The beating happened inside the White Elephant saloon at Thirteenth and Dodge, a place characterized as a "resort frequented by abandoned women." It seemed Dutch Jake met an unnamed woman to induce her to "to take up lodgings at his house," but Smith talked her out of it. That is when Swartz attacked. After Swartz paid his fines, he went after Smith and beat him again and "inside of two hours was back behind the bars." M.H. Curry, proprietor of the White Elephant, paid Swartz's $500 bail, and Dutch Jake was back on the streets. When Curry went to the police station to put up Swartz's bail, he found himself "arrested for keeping a disorderly house" and more fines to pay.

Widespread violence remained rampant, and at the end of December 1887, the *Bee* brought up Mike Phelan, who "called at the bawdy house of Mary Heiny," where he discovered all of the ladies were German. Phelan then sought "to show the superiority of Erin over Deutschland" and choked Louisa Schroetz "until she was black in the face" and then "kicked her out of doors." He then "took the next girl in order," but Officer Pulaski appeared to drag Phelan to jail.

Once again the *Bee* called on the city to "Close the Dens and Dives" in late December 1887, as the "high license law" would only succeed if the letter of the law was applied equally to the bawdy houses and notorious dens. The law stipulated licenses would be refused for those "known to be keepers of disorderly resorts," and the mayor and licensing board should follow through where "police court records and police officials furnish proof of the disreputable character of the applicant, or in the indecent and lawless conduct of the inmates of his resort." After all, as "long as dens, dives, and disorderly houses are tolerated" and licensed then "footpads, crooks and house-breakers will have harboring places," leaving everyone "exposed to burglary, robbery and violence." Truly, it seemed "high time that the lines were drawn" to separate the "reputable and decent" from the "strongholds of vice and crime." That's where "beastly orgies are kept up night and day, and where the professional outlaw always seeks and finds boon companionship and protection."

Omaha's metropolitan airs continued with construction of the New York Life Insurance Company building at 1650 Farnam Street. The ten-story building dominated Omaha's late nineteenth-century skyline and is now home to the Kutak Rock law firm. Equally impressive but lost to history was the new seven-story Bee Building built on the site of Ed Rosewater's home at Seventeenth and Farnam. All the while, the high times went on and on, and on January 1, 1888, the *Bee* reported a "falling out" between Lou Austin and Dora Conn, partners in a bawdy house. After the New Year's split, Lou was accused of taking fifteen dollars and twelve dollars' worth of clothes from Dora, who then "swore out a warrant" against her former partner. Lou Austin's trunk was found in a nearby alley where she had tried to hide it.

At the end of January 1888, the *Bee* described a "Cattle Man's Wild Freak" after stock dealer Thomas Lynch started out with $200 ready "to spend it all for liquor and a good time generally" in Omaha. He only spent $90 before he was "so crazy drunk" that he thought "people were after to rob him." He might not have been paranoid without reason, all things considered. It was in a Tenth Street saloon where Lynch "pulled out his revolver and commenced firing through the windows." His shots barely missed some people walking by. He then made his way, barely, out of the saloon to Mitchell's butcher shop. Lynch pointed his revolver at the butcher and "threatened to kill him" before Mitchell managed to get away and find a policeman who quickly "had the cattle man corralled."

There was another suicide in the *Bee* on February 1, 1888. It was "Rough on Rats" poison that time, and the newspaper gave the sad story of Addie Lamb. She came to Omaha from Avoca, Iowa, just three years before. Then, "last night she was lying dead in her home…dressed in a neatly-fitting brown silk walking suit and awaiting the tardy charity of her friends to furnish a coffin or a shroud." Lamb lived and died at 320 North Thirteenth Street, and the *Bee* called it "the old, old story," as she was "unable to withstand the temptations of a city life…[and] led astray." It seemed she had "more than once attempted to end a life that was distasteful to her" and this time was successful. In Omaha, she called herself Maud and was well known to those who visited the city's brothels. It was said that "those who seem to know her best speak most highly of her good qualities, but say they had the misfortune of drowning her sorrows in the wine cup." It seemed eight months or so before she returned from a trip to Grand Island and married bartender Charles Cummings. However, "fortune did not smile on the union" after Cummings lost his job. That "preyed upon the mind of his wife" and she returned "once or twice" to her previous occupation "only to be reclaimed by the husband." Eventually, Lamb became convinced "a dose of 'Rough On Rats,'" was the easiest "way to end her troubles." Help was sent for after she admitted what she had done, but "antidotes and remedies" proved useless, and she died at about seven o'clock in the morning. Lamb was only about twenty-four years old.

A week later, on February 7, the *Bee* announced the death of Mamie Brown. She "has been on the town for several years," and her body was taken to the undertaker. Brown died the day before, in the Bank's Building at Twelfth and Capitol. Her body was "awaiting the discovery of friends" from Omaha or from her home in Muscatine, Iowa. That issue also reported that Kate Bell, a madam of a brothel at Twelfth and Capitol, was released from jail. Bell was arrested for "disturbing the police" after "blowing a police whistle." She gave "the police a hard name" during her court appearance, with claims "they made her place a regular rendezvous when they should be on duty." She was caring for Mamie Brown—who was dying of consumption—when two "drunken fellows came into her place and became noisy and rough." That's when she blew the police whistle, trying to alert

An early twentieth-century view of Omaha's riverfront when the neighborhood just to the west grew even more notorious. *Courtesy of Chuck Martens.*

the authorities. Instead of helping, the officers "responded by running in, seizing her and dragging her off to jail" although she said she attempted "to explain matters" and "begged of them not to take her." As for Brown, who was "left without any care," she was "found dead in her bed." The judge released Kate Bell back into the world, despite the police alleging she was "crazy drunk" when arrested.

Sometimes the world was truly a "Courtesan's Fortune" as the *Bee* put it on March 1, 1888, and detailed an Omaha prostitute named Mattie Kollmeyer who was wanted in Sioux City—but not for the reasons you might expect. Instead, Kollmeyer had inherited up to $70,000, and "an intimate acquaintance" of a family named Stevens was trying to find her. Stevens told the *Bee* Kollmeyer "went to the bad" after the death of her husband, a Sioux City businessman, two years before. She went to Omaha and "entered a house of ill fame," where "her beauty and many accomplishments soon made her a favorite with frequenters of such resorts." It was said the "excitement of her life led her to drinking heavily and last July she was arrested, charged with drunkenness." It was also reported that her father was "a wealthy citizen of Sioux City, and survives his wife who has left her entire estate to her erring daughter" and that she should contact him via the *Bee*. Kollmeyer was "described as rather tall, slim, [with] dark hair and eyes" and "about" thirty-three years old. Stevens would not give out her married name.

Two days later, on March 3, the *Bee* labeled Kollmeyer "a shameless woman," as the police remained clueless while a *Bee* reporter found all about her and where she was living. The newspaper encouraged Mr. Stevens to come to the newspaper office and called her "shameful history" a "strange one." After the death of her husband, "a painter by trade," Kollmeyer "drifted into bad company, and was cast off by her father, a wealthy and respectable citizen." She went to Minneapolis and then Omaha, where her "life has been one of frightful degradation." When she came to town, she "entered a house of prostitution" at Eleventh and Davenport "kept by a woman named Flory." The newspaper claimed she was "addicted to drink" and when Kollmeyer was drunk she had a "most quarrelsome disposition." That had resulted in "many bloody fights," and she "figured frequently as a prisoner in police court" but it seems Kollmeyer often got away with a simple fine "promptly paid by friends in this city who knew her parents." All the while, she "drifted from one dive to another until her only companions were the lowest types," as she "was always to be found in the lowest haunts of vice, and here her vicious character was fully displayed by terrible debauches and many hard fights." It was early that winter when Kollmeyer "joined fortunes" with an unnamed black man and held a "mock marriage ceremony" before "the entire 'wedding' party got gloriously drunk." Right before Christmas, Mattie and her husband had moved to Fremont, Nebraska. It should be noted interracial marriage was illegal in Nebraska until the 1960s—although legal across the river in Iowa since 1851.

At the end of April, pilings for the new bridge across the Missouri River were started at Ninth and Douglas. The bridge opened that October and remained in use until 1966. In early May 1888, "Kansas City Liz" was back in court, and the *Bee* considered her "queen of the dusky cyprians in Omaha." She "waddled down to police court bareheaded in the rain" to ask Judge Berka "how much it would cost to whip a certain white woman." Liz claimed the woman had "alienated the affections of her late white lover, and she wished to wreck vengeance." She took the opportunity to bring up "some pretty hard charges" against a man she called Dick, a common thief and highwayman. Kansas City Liz claimed that the previous Saturday "he stole a pair of silk suspenders from a nice white gentleman 'caller' at her residence." After Kansas City Liz discovered Judge Berka "would charge her a good round sum for thrashing the white woman," she instead swore a warrant out against Dick.

The New York Life Insurance Company building at 1650 Farnam Street was Omaha's tallest building when completed in 1889. *Courtesy of Archives & Special Collections, Dr. C.C. and Mabel L. Criss Library, University of Nebraska at Omaha.*

A letter to the editor of the *Bee* from "Common Sense" was printed on September 2 and claimed, "The social evil cannot be suppressed in any large city." Omaha's "spasm" of reform to "break up houses of ill-fame and disperse the inmates of disorderly places" took place "in every community periodically without resulting in any good to anybody." The unnamed author, who might have been Rosewater, wrote of a "raid that was started some months ago by rowdies and libertines who had access to the columns of a certain newspaper in this city" with intentions of "levying blackmail." The effort was "backed by a Third ward councilman, who was elected by the aid of pimps and the lowest dregs of the Third ward, and who mingled with this class night and day." The unnamed Omaha councilman's "morals are based on a standard of cock and dog fighting and of other brutal sports which are patronized by the vilest and lowest of society." It sure seemed "rather amusing to see such a man stand in the council and pose as the champion of good morals." After all, the buildings surrounding the Dodge Street School were the California House hotel and stables, the Elkhorn Valley hotel, a tenement block and a grocery. For real reform, the entire neighborhood had to be emptied of disorderly places, and that meant scattering residents "all over the city into the respectable neighborhoods, where they will flourish, breed scandal and cause greater annoyance to respectable people than they do now." It was an open secret in Omaha that the children who went to the school were from the neighborhood "right in the midst of the worst haunts and dives." The "talk as to fines now imposed being license is mere bosh," as it was like "free whisky," and without fines, prostitution "would increase and multiply tenfold."

Then came Mayor Broatch's "War on the Bawdy Houses" announced by the *Bee* on September 5. The mayor instructed Chief Seavey to once again close down bordellos near schools. The mayor's instructions also noted to force the houses to be "inconspicuous as possible," with special attention toward "the low dives, especially those of mixed color," in order to drive them out. Miscegenation was frowned on in a city already well known as a place of designated districts.

There was another plea for social reform in the *Bee* on September 22 and a "crusade against the Third Ward dives." The newspaper also reported "two very pretty infants" were ready for adoption from the Temperance Union's "Open Door" at 2630 Davenport Street. That "Home for Unfortunates" was described by the *Bee* on October 28 as a "cozy and attractive brown cottage" that served as "a home for unfortunate young women…[and] refuge for young girls who have been entrapped in the snares of the seducer." It was also supposed to be a "training school for women who have been leading lives of shame but wish to reform and learn some self-supporting and honorable means of earning a livelihood." Six women sought refuge when the Open Door opened, and since that September, eighteen women had found their way to the Home for the Friendless. The Open Door was intended to aid "young women who have gone astray" so that they would "lead pure lives" and could remain until homes were secured far away from Omaha.

There were eighteen saloons listed in the 1889 city directory in the heart of Omaha's old Hell's Half Acre from Douglas north to Capitol between Ninth and Twelfth Streets. As one would suspect, a large number of women with unspecified professions were also listed in that same part of town. The city's national reputation seemed little improved, and in April 1889, the *Free Press* of San Marcos, Texas, claimed that Omaha received "about $20,000 from prostitution," with "more crime according to population than either Chicago or New York." It was a reputation perhaps well deserved. That April the *Bee* gave another example when William Nightingale enlisted two police officers for help with his "sad mission" of saving "his daughter from a house of ill repute." It seemed the Nightingale's eldest, a sixteen-year-old girl, was "keeping company with a fast crowd of young people" and "caused her parents no end of trouble." The girl went to a dance "in questionable quarters," and her father heard that she was in a Ninth Street bawdy house. He didn't find her and hoped she was "staying with friends." Then word came that his daughter was on Ninth Street, and the mistress of the place had lied. Nightingale sought help from police, only to find his daughter at Pearl Mock's, where she was found sitting "on a sofa near the center of the room, surrounded by painted sirens and disreputable men, dressed to render her charms conspicuous…receiving the caresses of a frequenter of the bagnio." The men ran out when the police appeared, leaving Nightingale alone with his daughter. That seemed enough, as the "girl was completely overcome, and with one cry, fell fainting into her father's arms," which left the "tittering wantons" to help "in restoring her to consciousness." Nightingale then left with her father.

On April 13, 1889, the *Bee* reported all the furniture from the Wilson-Branch mansion on Lower Douglas had been sold at a public auction for $300. The "halls and rooms of the structure are deserted and drear, the inmates have been dispersed throughout the city and country." This "palace" was constructed about eight years before by gambler Dan Allen, and "a life interest was given to Miss Annie Wilson." It was then said that after her

A rare 1898 view of Farnam east of Sixteenth Street. The old Douglas County Courthouse (*right*) was where many spent longer than a night in the basement jail. *Courtesy of Archives & Special Collections, Dr. C.C. and Mabel L. Criss Library, University of Nebraska at Omaha.*

death the property would revert to Dan's brother Ethan, who lived about forty miles from the city. Instead, the house reopened, and something else happened in the end.

There was a "terrible charge" by Nettie Everd of Chicago in the *Bee* at the end of April against the "notorious bawdy house proprietor" known as "French Em." Everd was twenty-two years old, and in the two years since her father's death, she had worked as a housekeeper in Chicago. Then she met Joe Liberty, and in two weeks, he convinced her to go to Omaha to make more money. Once in the city, Liberty took Everd to French Em's, where it didn't take long for her to figure out "what kind of a place" she was in. Everd was "prevented" from leaving, and a "close watch was kept over her to prevent her escape." After that, Everd "was forced, through threats, to carry on the nefarious business of the bawdy house" until she escaped out the basement. She went to the police and "swore out a warrant for French Em's arrest, and will also file an information against Joe Liberty." Then, after Judge Berka determined to send Everd to the Temperance Union's Open Door, she had "a vigorous kick." The *Bee* quoted her saying "No 'Open Door' for me....I'm too old a chicken for that." She then asked Officer Pulaski "Say, Count...what do you take me for anyway?" Then, poor, innocent Everd

Jobbing houses and warehouses like these gradually supplanted the collection of brothels and cribs. Only the building on the right at Eleventh and Harney remains standing. *Courtesy of Archives & Special Collections, Dr. C.C. and Mabel L. Criss Library, University of Nebraska at Omaha.*

"launched off into a tirade of bawdy house slang that made some of the hardened policemen blush" and was sent to jail.

That same issue of the *Bee* noted that several people who lived or owned property near Ninth and Dodge asked the police "to suppress certain bawdy houses." The suspicious houses in question were located at 806, 808, 812, 814 and 818 Dodge Street and Omaha police sergeant Sigwart was sent "to see if the places are actually houses of ill fame." If so, "the inmates will be ordered to vacate by May 5."

Then, near the last day of December 1889, the *Bee* gave details on a soldier from Fort Omaha named Frank Carson who "floated into the slums on Sunday night" and intended on "whooping her up." Carson's first visit was to a dive run by the Kansas City Liz. Carson claimed that "as soon as he stepped into the door Liz grabbed two rings from his fingers" and wouldn't give them back. On the other hand, Liz said "Carson gave her the rings," and a "lively row ensued" that ended when the two of them were arrested for disturbing the peace.

6

The Man-Landlady

The rough-and-tumble 1880s gave way to a new decade of debauchery, as Omaha continued its growth into a stolid midwestern city. By 1890, Omaha claimed to be one of America's largest twenty-five cities, with a reputed population of just over 140,000 people. The sordid city even achieved national prominence before the decade ended. In 1890, residents could point with pride at construction of Omaha's new city hall next to the Bee Building at Sixteenth and Farnam, complete with a miniature Statue of Liberty on top. At the same time, the city remained a place where exploitation and abuse were common. On March 29, 1890, the *Bee* gave the details of an abusive man named M.E. Lowry, a "very red-headed young loafer," who was hauled in by police for assaulting his wife. Seven months earlier, Lowry married "a woman of the town," and they agreed—according to the wife—that he "should earn a living and the two would live as respectable people." However, soon after the wedding, he "refused to work" and instead "insisted on his bride entering a house of shame." With that, the newlywed Mrs. Lowry "began boarding with Madam Kelley" at the corner of Ninth and Capitol. Then Lowry showed up one night when Kelley was asleep and "demanded of the madam to produce his wife." She told him his wife was "about the house somewhere." Lowry's response, as printed by the *Bee*, was, "If you don't produce her I'll burn the place down." Kelley "was not to be bluffed" and ran him out with a hatchet. He returned later, but she wouldn't give him money so he "assaulted her brutally." He was arrested, and Mrs. Lowry told the newspaper she had "been compelled to support him ever since they were married" but refused to continue.

One prominent addition to Omaha's history of vice was the Castle, constructed by M.F. Martin in 1891 on the northwest corner of Ninth and Dodge. Nominally a furniture dealer, during the 1890s, Martin emerged as kingpin of Omaha vice who was eventually damned by Josie Washburn as the "Man-Landlady." Half of Martin's new Castle was a hotel, and by June 1894, the other half was rented as a brothel for $200 a month. That tawdry detail came to light when the *Bee* detailed Omaha's "Padrone System." It seemed nothing but outright extortion, as Martin and his wife then owned almost all the property in Omaha's "Burnt District," as old Hell's Half Acre was then known.

Martin's "bawdy houses of various degrees of pretension" lined three blocks of Ninth Street from Douglas north to Capitol and then west. One old two-story brick building at Ninth and Douglas was "said to be in very poor condition" but rented for $175 a month. The tenant was responsible for "gas, water, repairs, etc." along with their monthly fines. Worse were the six "one-story brick flats" at Ninth and Dodge that were rented for $3 a day to "women of the most degraded character." The newspaper described each as having three rooms, none "much more than large enough to turn around in," with an eight- by ten-foot parlor with "cheap carpet, sheet iron stove,… [and a] bedroom furnished with a cheap chamber set" that led "into a sort of kitchen that is not furnished at all."

The Overland hotel, on the second and third floors of the building at Thirteenth and Howard, seems the last of the sort of small hotels once common across downtown Omaha. *Author's collection.*

The newspaper went on to describe over forty more establishments Martin owned, with rent ranging from $2.50 a day and up. Among them was the three-story wooden building "constructed in the cheapest manner possible" at Ninth and Dodge that was rented to Lottie Lee for $200 a month. Martin owned seventeen houses of prostitution alone on the north side of Capitol between Ninth and Tenth Streets that were inhabited by "courtesans of the most abandoned descriptions." Martin's other properties ranged from three-story brick buildings to one-story frame shanties. Martin openly boasted of his clout in the city and ability to drive any woman out of town who wouldn't "submit to his extortions in the matter of rents and furniture deals."

The 1890s also brought Tom Dennison to Omaha. The Iowa-born gambler would eventually control almost every aspect of vice with a political machine inherited from Ed Rosewater that dominated Omaha until 1933. Professor Orville Menard, who recognized the relationship between Rosewater, the *Bee* and Dennison's rise to power, noted when Dennison moved to town, the city limits of what was tolerated ran from Cass Street south to Jackson and from the Missouri River west to Fifteenth Street. Petty crime remained common, including two burglaries described by the *Bee* in September 1894. The porter at Jennings's resort at Ninth and Capitol scared them off, but a candy store on South Thirteenth Street was robbed of around eight dollars' worth of candy and gum. Police suspected it was boys living in the neighborhood.

In mid-December 1895, the *Bee* announced the fifteen-year-old St. Elmo theater was condemned and would be razed. The newspaper recounted its notorious history while Jack Nugent gambled away his profits and, at last account, was a motorman driving a Chicago streetcar. In its last years, the once notorious theater was used to store carriages. The St. Elmo was gone, but entertainment of a similar sort remained. One establishment of that era pointed out in the Omaha WPA guide was the Nebraska Music Hall at 1307 Douglas Street, described as a place of "cheap cigars, beer, vulgar sketches, and the display of personal charms by the women performers."

The *Bee* went on another crusade in early February 1897 against liquor and lewd women with details that liquor licenses were granted to places that weren't saloons but instead something else, contrary to Nebraska law. The proprietors and their addresses were duly listed by the newspaper:

- *Ruby Smith at 111 South Ninth*
- *Nora Hull at 116 South Ninth*
- *Minnie Fairchild at 120 South Ninth*
- *May Coleman at 117 North Ninth*

- *Lillian Morton at 115 North Ninth*
- *Georgie Ward at 123 North Ninth*
- *Edna Stewart at 101 North Ninth*
- *Jettie Reynolds at 116-188 North Ninth*
- *Sadie Jennings at 114 North Ninth*
- *Anna Wilson at 110–112 North Ninth*
- *Olive Branch at 108 North Ninth*
- *Mamie Brown at 909 Capitol*
- *Bertie Mann at 905 Capitol*
- *Anna Wilson at 910–912 Douglas*
- *Grace Walton at 822 Dodge Street*

The next year, Omaha hosted the grandiose Trans-Mississippi Exposition at what is now Kountze Park. The five-month event put Omaha on the map and brought millions of people, including President McKinley and Geronimo. It was a celebratory spectacle that has yet to be surpassed in the city. The event seemed an affirmation of American might and prosperity, as it took place during and just after the four-month-long Spanish-American War, which established the country as a world power. The exposition at Omaha also brought sports for all sorts, including dancer Little Egypt and Little Miss Chicago, who would appear that July at the Gaiety theater at Fifteenth and Capitol.

Omaha's 1899 Great American Exposition wasn't as successful, as the city's wide-open side continued unabated into the twentieth century. Omaha claimed almost 103,000 people by 1900 and still had a dubious reputation. In May 1904, the *Herald* newspaper out in Alliance, Nebraska, called Omaha a "haven of rest," as the city had "long been a rendezvous for protected thieves, robbers, porch climbers, and burglars."

The talk around Omaha and in the *Bee* in November 1905 was potential construction by M.E. Smith & Company of a "mammoth wholesale dry goods house and factory" on Ninth between Douglas and Farnam. The Nash Block, now the Greenhouse apartments, is the only remnant of Jobber's Canyon, as the old vice district was replaced with factories for food production and massive warehouses of goods ready to be shipped throughout the West. The *Bee* believed more industry would follow the new Ninth Street railroad tracks and "encroach on the red light district" until the prostitutes were "forced to find other locations."

As Omaha's old designated district of vice became something else, in 1906, Democrat James "Cowboy Jim" Dahlman was elected to his first term as mayor with support from Dennison's nominally Republican machine. Dahlman had fled Texas after killing his brother-in-law and ended up a

Only tobacco and candy were said to be sold in this postcard of what used to be the notorious Castle at Ninth and Dodge. *Courtesy of Chuck Martens.*

cowboy in Chadron, Nebraska, before he entered politics. He and his wife moved to Omaha in 1898, and he served as mayor of the city from 1906 to 1917 and again from 1922 until he died in office in 1930.

By 1907, M.F. Martin had established himself as a real estate agent, with his land deals and building permits in the newspaper like any other Omaha businessman. In November and December that year, the real source of his wealth was spilled through the pages of the Omaha's *Bee* and *World-Herald*, with questions over the sanitary conditions of the Arcade. For reasons known to Mayor Dahlman—and likely Tom Dennison—an inquiry into the conduct of the chief of police opened up, with Martin the apparent target. The mayor and two members of the Board of Fire and Police Commissioners paid an evening

All sorts of transportation can be seen in 1906 in front of the Union Pacific passenger depot, which stood at Tenth and Marcy from 1899 until 1931. In the background can be seen the 1898 Burlington passenger depot, still standing and much modified. *Courtesy of Chuck Martens.*

visit to the Arcade, and the *Bee* reported they found the cribs not hooked up to the sewer but instead "outhouses in all stages of dilapidation."

Martin had enough influence to avoid arrest, but on December 6, the *World-Herald* called it a "first step" following his admission he was a "regular contributor to charity" through police channels or, in short, payoffs and kickbacks. Three days later, the Omaha Anti-Saloon League was organized, and on December 12, 1907, the front page of the *World-Herald* was all about Martin's apparent generosity toward the police department.

Two days later, on December 14, the *Bee* reported police raided Martin's Arcade and closed the "notorious resort." That was front-page news, as Judge Crawford issued warrants against the women as well as M.F. Martin and his collector of rents. The judge was quoted by the *Bee* saying he didn't "want to arrest these poor women who have been selling their bodies to pay Martin toll." A mad scramble started after residents heard they would be "pinched" with their belongings "tied up in pillow shams, sheets, and the like and carried in bundles." The next day, the *Bee* reported a "motley and cosmopolitan" crowd with sixty women in court with warrants issued for twenty more. They all pleaded guilty and paid the five-dollar fine. The women included "every nationality of Europe and Asia, almost." One told the newspaper it was winter, and they were "thrown

No one knows how many times this scene was played out in Omaha and was perhaps staged by this unnamed couple in 1910. *Courtesy of Special Collections, the Durham Museum.*

out of our rooms without a minute's notice" with nowhere to go. The judge told them they could return for their belongings, but the "iron doors" of the Arcade were "locked with a padlock." Martin was fined one hundred dollars for renting property at 808 Dodge Street "for immoral purposes," while the case against John Harris, who collected the rent, was dismissed. The newspaper was unsure of Martin's plans, as the Arcade and all other nearby brothels he owned were emptied out. What Martin did was build the cribs up to two stories and get around the ordinance. They were dubbed "made-over buildings" by the *Bee* in October 1908. Two months later, in December, the Omaha grand jury turned its attention to the obscene pictures sold with packs of cigarettes.

Seemingly disgusted with the same old–same old, in 1909 Josie Washburn published *Underworld Sewer* about her experiences—with vice in general and Omaha in particular—after almost forty years in the business. Her book was advertised in the *Bee* that October and available for $1.50, first at Swartz & McIlvey's at 109 South Fifteenth, and then at "all bookstores."

Washburn called the events of 1907 the "one-year war" and castigated M.F. Martin as the "Man Landlady." To her, it was a "farce" orchestrated by the

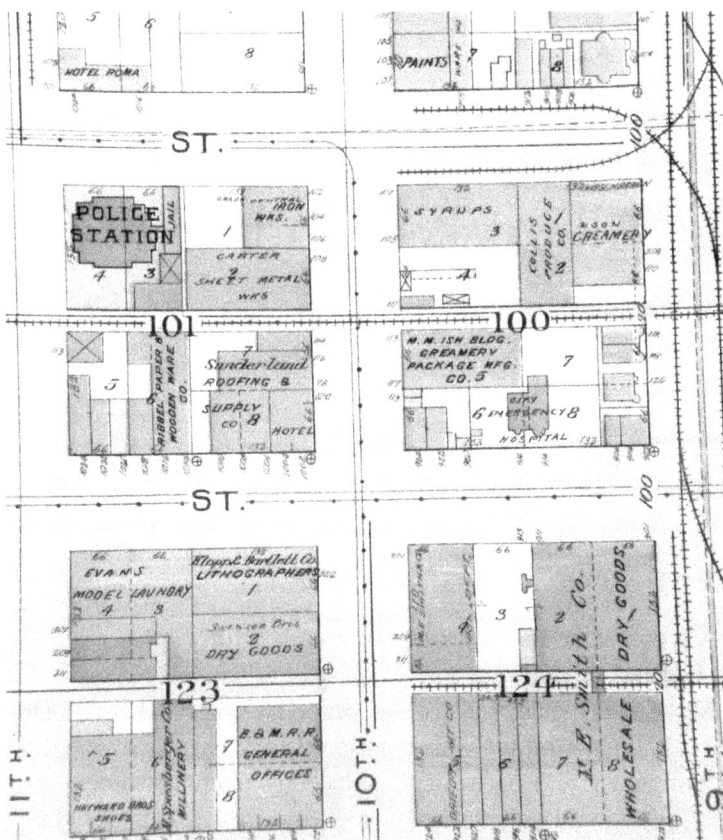

Anna Wilson's brothel was the City Emergency Hospital on this 1918 map. A block north, the distinctive Castle was still on the corner, and the Dodge Street School was the police station. Also, note the general offices of the B&M Railroad, which still stand at Tenth and Farnam Streets. *Courtesy of Archives & Special Collections, Dr. C.C. and Mabel L. Criss Library, University of Nebraska at Omaha.*

newspapers, Dennison and others for their own benefit. She described the bright electric lights as the only modernization in the cribs, which were just "two small rooms, about six feet high; a door and a window forms the whole front." That was for obvious visibility and built with a "scalloped appearance" designed "to be artistic," as potential customers could easily browse by to find what they wanted. There were also an "electric push-button" between the Arcade cribs and an adjacent saloon and restaurant also owned by M.F. Martin. Washburn, who saw much and believed anyone with syphilis should be registered, wrote, a "girl who goes wrong is not so much to blame for her sin as those who create or permit the condition." There was always that "instinct for self-preservation," but there was no reform in Omaha, just "persecution and imprisonment."

7
The Albert Law and Afterward

The Union Pacific moved its headquarters out of the Herndon House in 1911 when last call came for Omaha's designated neighborhood of vice. By late May 1911, the city seemed determined to enforce Alberts's Disorderly House Act and close up the wide-open bordellos. The *Bee* reported on April 8 that "temporary and permanent injunctions against disorderly houses as nuisances" would end, as property owners and their agents would be "liable for the fines and taxes imposed" that, "in discretion of the court," ranged from $200 up to $1,000. Not even M.F. Martin could afford to raise the rent that high.

By 1911, Omaha's police headquarters and jail had moved into the old Dodge Street School that had provided so much political fodder over the years. It was the city jail where the "worst of all nations arrive at one time or another." There, "day after day," were housed the

> *old soak and young desperado, lost woman and devitalized man, shrinking venturers in wickedness and plumed bravados of the demi-monde, unfortunate working women and penniless wanderers, hot-tempered killers and victims of cruel circumstance, crafty thieves and bungling check workers, desperate burglars and sneaking holdups, strong fighting men and cowardly wife beaters.*

The injunction against the Albert Law was lifted in early June although the *Bee* assured readers the "resorts in the pink section of town" had time for "French leave" before prosecution. The lawyers seemed to have profited most, and not everyone knew about it. On July 24, 1911, the *Bee* reported

The City Hospital in Anna Wilson's former brothel is shown on the left next to a Deep Rock gas station in this 1930 view of Douglas looking east of Tenth Street. *Courtesy of Special Collections, the Durham Museum.*

Albert Brown visited the city from Honey Creek, Iowa, only to find his "favorite haunt," Clara White's at 110 North Ninth Street, "closed and padlocked." Brown busted out the windows and ripped the bars off the doors before the police arrived and arrested him for destroying property.

In August 1911, Omaha's *Daily News* reported seventy-six-year-old Anna Wilson was worth upward of $1 million. It was said she had retired years before to Wirt Street and intended to donate her Douglas Street brothel as a public hospital. Her last will, printed by the *News* on September 15, 1911, dispensed her wealth across Omaha, including to Prospect Hill cemetery, the Omaha City Mission, the Old People's Home, the Creche home for the unfortunate, the Child Saving Institute, Associated Charities and Clarkson and Wise Memorial Hospital. She died the next month at her home at 2018 Wirt Street. Health commissioner Connell was quoted by the *Bee* in October 1911 as saying that $3,500 was needed to "repair and equip" the city's new emergency hospital in Wilson's old brothel and thought Douglas County should pay half.

The warehouses had replaced the cribs in this early twentieth-century postcard view looking north from Tenth and Jackson. *Courtesy of Chuck Marten.*

Such bucolic early twentieth-century views of Capitol Avenue looking west toward Omaha High School are common. Rarer seem to be any images of Capitol east of Twelfth Street. *Courtesy of Chuck Marten.*

By the end of November 1911, all of M.F. Martin's remaining "red light property" was up for sale, including the remnants of the Arcade with its second stories added to avoid the crib ordinance. Also for sale were ten lots

This unnamed woman photographed in Omaha in 1913 was a telephone operator, one of the few legitimate options for women seeking employment. *Courtesy of Special Collections, the Durham Museum.*

along Ninth between Douglas and Capitol offered as "trackage property." There had been no income from those properties since the Albert Law.

Naturally, this just dispersed Omaha vice, with estimates of the number of prostitutes in Omaha ranging up to 2,600 women spread across downtown by the Albert Law. By April 1914, the *Bee* witnessed "further purifying" after legal action was taken against the owners of the lots used as "places of immorality."

One place noted was 1710 North Sixteenth Street, "raided several times by police." Meanwhile, M.F. Martin sold the corner of Eighteenth and Dodge to Gordon-Lawless in June 1914, which the *Bee* considered "another step in the transition" from vice into the "realm of wholesaling and manufacturing." All the while, Tom Dennison's political organization did its best to fix every election, including helping orchestrate the 1919 courthouse riot during which William D. Brown was lynched in front of the Douglas County Courthouse and his body burned in the middle of Seventeenth and Dodge. It was all to make the reform government look bad and bring Dennison's bunch back into office. It worked—for awhile—and Dahlman was reelected as mayor.

The old Herndon House was torn down in 1922, while Tom Dennison ensured there was no real prohibition of alcohol in Omaha, at least as long as everyone paid. Still, in 1933, Dennison's political machine was finally defeated shortly before his death. The WPA guide to Omaha of the 1930s dubbed Douglas between Twelfth and Fourteenth as "Pawnshop Row" and a place of "cheap hotels, eating houses, pawnshops, and second-hand stores." The City Emergency Hospital in Anna Wilson's old brothel then had forty-six beds for contagious diseases and a venereal clinic with six nurses and an intern on duty. In 1936, the one-time Diamond gambling house at 1313 Douglas Street was razed as the Great Depression filled the sidewalks with homeless hobos, bums, tramps and transients of every sorts who ended up in Omaha off the road or boxcar.

Dennison's void was soon filled by all sorts of up-and-comers, with bookmakers like Max Abramson and Casey Gaughan and others like Bennie "the Blimp" Barone who might have been something more. Anything was possible with Meyer Lanksy's Kennel Club greyhound racing track running across the river in Council Bluffs and Kansas City mobster Charles Binaggio looking around for a cut. That new era revolved around cigar stores and swanky nightclubs with prostitutes easily available at the Bell Hotel at 1421 Dodge. There was a brief mention in the *World-Herald* in January 1944 about the old days as 901–5 Capitol Avenue was torn down. The last resident was an old man evicted just before demolition. Two years later, in April 1946, Anna Wilson's brothel-turned-hospital was razed as a landmark of a different sort of city.

Nowadays, Omaha gambling is limited to pickle cards, simulcast racing at Horseman's Park and keno, while three casinos across the river in Council Bluffs offer almost everything else. Anna Wilson remains remembered as a city benefactor. The prominent grave at Prospect Hill cemetery she shares with Dan Allen remains a city landmark. Josie Washburn's account found new life after her book was reprinted in the 1990s. Still, Josie's ultimate fate, like most of the women and men mentioned, remains unknown.

Bibliography

BOOKS

DeVol, George. *Forty Years a Gambler on the Mississippi*. Cincinnati, OH: DeVol & Haines, 1887.

Menard, Orville. *River City Empire: Tom Dennison's Omaha*. Lincoln: University of Nebraska Press, 1989.

Miller, Linda. *Omaha: A Guide to the City and Environs*. Omaha, NE: Omaha Public Library, 1981.

Washburn, Josie. *The Underworld Sewer: A Prostitute Reflects on Life in the Trade, 1871–1909*. Omaha, NE: Washburn Publishing, 1909. Reprinted with introduction by Sharon E. Wood. Lincoln: University of Nebraska Press, 1997.

DIRECTORIES

Wolfe's Omaha Directory for 1874–1875.
Wolfe's Omaha Directory for 1879–1880.
Wolfe's Omaha Directory for 1889–1890.

BIBLIOGRAPHY

NEWSPAPERS

Alliance Herald
New York Times
New York Tribune
Omaha Daily Bee
Omaha Daily News
Omaha World-Herald

About the Author

Ryan Roenfeld is a fifth-generation resident of Mills County, Iowa, and former president of the Historical Society of Pottawattamie County. He is the author or coauthor of several books on the history of southwest Iowa and, at present, teaches continuing education classes on Omaha history for Omaha's Metropolitan Community College and is a full-time student at the University of Nebraska at Omaha.

www.ingramcontent.com/pod-product-compliance
Lightning Source LLC
Chambersburg PA
CBHW060651150426

42813CB00052B/586

* 9 7 8 1 5 4 0 2 1 5 5 4 3 *